ASPEN TO GLENWOOD

Day Hikes IN THE
Roaring Fork
Valley and
Beyond

WARREN OHLRICH

WHO PRESS • BASALT, COLORADO

PUBLISHED BY

WHO Press
www.whopress.com

Library of Congress Control Number: 2004106781

ISBN 978-1-882426-20-1

Printed in the United States of America

Interior photos by Karen B. Ohlrich & Warren H. Ohlrich
Photo p. 117 by Karen Smith
Cover photos by Karen B. Ohlrich

Cover design by Curt Carpenter
Interior maps by Warren H. Ohlrich
Back cover map by Curt Carpenter

Table of Contents

Introduction 5

Wilderness 7

Wilderness Ethics 7

Independence Pass 9
  1. Difficult Trail 11
  2. Weller Lake 12
  3. Grottos 13
  4. Braille Trail & Discovery Trail 15
  5. New York Creek Trail 16
  6. Grizzly Lake 18
  7. Anderson & Petroleum Lakes 19
  8. Midway Pass 21
  9. Linkins Lake 22
  10. Lost Man Loop 23
  11. Continental Divide 26

Aspen 29
  12. Rio Grande Trail 29
  13. Ute Trail 31
  14. Smuggler Mountain 32
  15. Hunter Valley 34
  16. Hunter Creek–Smuggler Loop 35
  17. Sunnyside–Hunter Valley Loop 38
  18. American Lake 41
  19. Cathedral Lake/Electric Pass......................................42
  20. Crater Lake 45
  21. Buckskin Pass 46
  22. West Maroon Pass 48

Snowmass Village/Snowmass 51
  23. Sleigh Ride Trail 51
  24. Nature Trail 52

25. Ditch Trail 53

26. East Snowmass Trail 54

27. Rim Trail 56

28. Government Trail 58

29. Capitol Creek Loop 62

30. Hell Roaring Trail 64

31. Snowmass Creek Trail (Maroon–Snowmass Trail) ... 66

Basalt/Fryingpan 69

32. Arbaney–Kittle Trail 71

33. Rocky Fork Trail 72

34. Ruedi Overlook Trail 74

35. Josephine Lake 75

36. Savage Lakes 78

37. Lyle & Mormon Lakes 79

38. Fryingpan Lakes 82

Carbondale/Redstone/Marble 85

39. Mushroom Rock Trail 86

40. Thomas Lakes 88

41. Thompson Creek Trail 89

42. Perham Creek Trail 90

43. Avalanche Creek Trail 93

44. East Creek Trail 94

45. Buckskin Basin/Avalanche Pass 96

46. Geneva Lake 98

47. Ragged Mountain Trail 100

Glenwood Springs 103

48. Doc Holliday Trail 103

49. Red Mountain Trail 105

50. Jess Weaver Trail 106

51. Grizzly Creek Trail 108

52. Hanging Lake 110

Index 112

Introduction

*A**spen to Glenwood* was written to be a comprehensive trail guide for day hikes in the Central Colorado area that includes: Independence Pass; the Roaring Fork Valley from Aspen to Glenwood Springs; the Fryingpan River Valley to the Continental Divide; the Crystal River Valley from Carbondale to Redstone, Marble, and McClure Pass; and the Glenwood Canyon corridor near Glenwood Springs. Some of the trails are repeats of trails, or portions of trails, in *Aspen–Snowmass Trails* and *Aspen and Central Colorado Trails*, but many are lesser known trails, or have not previously been included in any hiking guides. All of these trails are maintained, but not always heavily traveled.

As always, I have hiked each trail anew, carefully recording notes, to be able to give the latest information necessary to make the hike a safe and enjoyable one, and to give insights as to what to expect. The information in this book is up-to-date and gathered through my own experience. As many of you may know, I am a stickler for details on how to get to the trailheads, and how to keep on the correct route throughout a hike.

Various other aids, besides this guide, can be helpful on your trip. The USGS 7½-minute topographic maps and the *Trails Illustrated* maps are listed for each route. The routes in this guide are described well enough so that a map is not absolutely necessary, but they do give a good perspective of where you are—again, an extra security tool. The maps in the books are only there to give you an overall picture of where the trails and trailheads are located.

Although not everyone has a GPS (global positioning system), GPS coordinates have been included for all trailheads and destinations, and for any points on the route that may be critical to the navigation for the trip. A GPS is not necessary to hike the trails in this book—the trail route directions are sufficient—but having a GPS provides extra security and safety for the hiker. And, it's also fun to see how far it is to the next point, or whether you are really at the spot that you think you are. To determine the GPS coordinates for this book, I have used the WGS84 Map Datum and the UTM metric grid system. When comparing these coordinates with a position on the USGS 7½-minute topographic maps (which use the 1927 Map Datum), you will find that the WGS84 Map Datum readings show 200 meters north of the corresponding position on the USGS map, and the GPS altitude reading is usually slightly higher.

As in my other guide books, I have included sections on "Wilderness" and "Wilderness Ethics", since many of the trails are in designated Wilderness. You can familiarize yourself with the current Wilderness regulations by visiting the Forest Service offices and by reading signs at the trailheads. Although some of the ethics and regulations are for backpacking and camping, they are included in case you also extend some of these trips into backpacking trips.

Since virtually all of these hikes are in the Colorado backcountry, a number of precautions should be taken. Pace yourself and realize that times in this guide do not include extended stops. The difficulty factors are subjective—for any one hiker the route could actually be more difficult than rated in the guide, especially if you are not accustomed to the altitude and backcountry conditions. Be aware that dizziness, headaches, lack of appetite, and nausea are signs of altitude sickness. Start your hike early in the day—sudden thunderstorms in the afternoon are almost a daily event during the summer in these mountains, even if the sky is clear early in the day. For this reason, it's necessary to carry rain gear and extra clothing on all but the shortest hikes. Many of the high altitude trails will be snow-covered well into the summer, often into July, so be sure to check with the Forest Service on trail conditions for these hikes.

Carry an adequate supply of water (about one pint per person for each three miles); you cannot drink water from any of the streams without filtering it, because of giardia, a microscopic organism that can make you very sick. Keep dry and warm when hiking—hypothermia is a lowering of the body's core temperature which can lead to death.

For maps, information, gear, and clothing, Ute Mountaineer in Aspen, Bristlecone Mountain Sports in Basalt, and Summit Canyon Mountaineering in Glenwood Springs are all well stocked and well informed.

I would like to thank the Forest Service for their input into this hiking guide. Thanks also to Kristine Tracz and my wife, Karen, for accompanying me on many of these hikes as I hiked and re-hiked the trails. Address any comments, corrections, suggestions, or inquiries concerning this guide to: Warren H. Ohlrich, 0311 West Sopris Creek Rd., Basalt, CO 81621.

Enjoy hiking here in one of the most beautiful areas in the country!

Wilderness

Since the late 1800s selected public lands have been protected from uncontrolled development and reserved to benefit the Nation as a whole. This process has been formalized in The Wilderness Act of 1964. Objectives for preserving the wilderness system include: perpetuating a long-lasting system of high quality wilderness that represents natural ecosystems; providing opportunities for public use and enjoyment of the wilderness resource; allowing plants and animals indigenous to the area to develop through natural processes; maintaining watersheds and airsheds in a healthy condition; protecting threatened or endangered plant and animal species. User comfort is not an objective—Wilderness exists for its own intrinsic values. Wilderness areas are in a delicate state of natural balance, they are not a renewable resource.

Four Wilderness areas are covered in this guide: Maroon Bells–Snowmass Wilderness, Hunter–Fryingpan Wilderness, Holy Cross Wilderness, and Collegiate Peaks Wilderness.

Wilderness Ethics

LESSEN YOUR IMPACT

Limit the size of your group. Limit group sizes to 10 people. Groups under 10 people have less impact on the Wilderness.

Shortcuts cause erosion. Please stay on the established trail which is designed to minimize erosion, protect vegetation, and maintain a comfortable grade.

Leave rocks, flowers, wood, antlers, and other interesting items in their natural state for others to enjoy. Picking wildflowers is punishable by law. "Take only memories, leave only footprints."

Do not feed wildlife. Your food or leftovers can upset the natural balance of their food chain or cause bacteria harmful to them.

Watch your step—the alpine tundra is delicate. Above timber line, walk on trails, rocks, or snow when possible.

Leave mechanization behind. Use of motorized/mechanical transport and equipment (including mountain bikes) within the Wilderness is prohibited. Mountain bikes are allowed on most non-Wilderness trails.

ANIMALS IN THE BACKCOUNTRY

Keep dogs on a leash at all times. Their presence can disrupt wildlife and disturb other users of the Wilderness. You are encouraged to leave your dogs or other pets at home. Keep dogs out of sandy, gravelly bottoms 18 inches or less deep, especially near inlets and outlets, in high altitude lakes so they don't disturb spawning grounds for the trout.

Do not hobble, picket, or tether horses within 100 feet of lakes, streams, and trails. This helps keep lakes and streams clean and pure.

CAMPING

Camp only on hard ground at least 100 feet away from streams, lakes, and trails. Use existing sites when possible. This will reduce your impact on the environment and increase your privacy. Vegetation and soils adjacent to lakes and streams are extremely sensitive to disturbance. Respect "No Camping Here" or "Closed for Revegetation" signs.

Use a lightweight backpacking stove instead of building a campfire. Campfires leave a permanent scar on rocks and soil. Gas stoves don't deplete your Wilderness wood-fuel resources, especially in the high country above 10,000 feet, where wood is being burned faster than it's produced. Gas stoves are required above timber line.

Wash at least 100 feet away from water source and throw out dirty water away from water source. Use biodegradable soap. Don't wash or bathe in the lake or stream; even biodegradable soap pollutes if it goes directly into the water.

Keep your noise level low. Unnecessary loud noise may frighten wildlife and annoy other Wilderness visitors.

Pack out what you pack in. Leave no trace. Please pick up anyone else's trash you may find along the way. Leave your campsite in a natural state. Remember, aluminum and plastic don't burn!

SANITATION

Bury feces. Use a small trowel to bury human waste 6–8 inches deep and at least 100 feet away from water sources and trails. Pack out your toilet paper in a plastic bag.

Others have passed this way before, others will again...treat the Wilderness as forever.

Independence Pass

The road climbing 4,000 feet from Aspen to Independence Pass (12,095 feet) on the Continental Divide was once the main route for prospectors and miners coming to Aspen from Leadville and beyond to strike it rich in the silver mines. The journey was treacherous, and many wagons never made it all the way to Aspen. Even today, the road is closed most of the year because of the deep snows. But now, from Memorial Day to late October, the paved Highway 82 leads to a wealth of outdoor activities, especially hiking, on the western flank of the Continental Divide, most of which is Wilderness. The drive is spectacular, as is the scenery, which is highlighted by lakes, peaks, rushing creeks, rock formations, and magnificent vistas. The ghost town of Independence, where gold was discovered on July 4, 1879, is still visible just a few miles west of the pass.

Hikes #1–4 lie closer to Aspen and are relatively easy, with the Grottos (#3) being more of a picnic and exploration area than a real hike. The Braille Trail & Discovery Trail (#4) and Weller Lake (#2) offer good introductions to the outdoor world for young and old alike. The Difficult Trail (#1) lures the hiker a little deeper into the Wilderness to explore its beauty.

Hikes #5–7 are accessed by an old mining road that leads along the roaring Lincoln Creek into a remote valley, once resplendent with mining activity. These hikes take you to lakes and ridges deep in the Wilderness, combining a scenic drive with some challenging hiking.

Hikes #8–11 make close contact with the Continental Divide itself, exploring alpine lakes and passes with spectacular views of the Divide. Hike #11 goes right along the ridge of the Divide. These are definitely high altitude hikes, not for those who have not yet acclimated to the altitude.

1. Difficult Trail

Start/Finish: Day Use Parking Lot at Difficult Campground
(8,140 feet; 13S0346659E, 4334089N)
Destination: End of maintained trail (9,500 feet, 13S0346863E,
4331178N)
Round Trip: 6–7 miles / 4 hours
Difficulty: Moderate (parts of the trail are quite steep)
Elevation Range: 8,140–9,500 feet
Maps: USGS Aspen, Hayden Peak; TI #127
Wilderness Designation: Collegiate Peaks Wilderness

General Comments: This forested trail offers a wide range of hiking
experiences, including a peaceful forest walk, good views of the Roaring
Fork Valley, the roar and excitement of the bouldered Difficult Creek,
and the remains of cabins from the mining days. Occasionally
adventurous hikers will try to keep going to find a way to the top of
Aspen Mountain, but the route is overgrown and no real route exists. The
trailhead is only 4 miles from Aspen, and is very convenient for campers
at Difficult Campground, where the trail begins.

Directions to Trailhead: Take Highway 82 east from Aspen for 4
miles (.2 miles past 45 mile marker) and turn right into Difficult
Campground. Go .6 miles down the road to the Day Use parking area on
the right. The trail starts in the back left corner of the lot.

Trail Route: Follow the trail out of the parking lot, staying left at an
immediate fork, for several hundred feet through brush and willow, cross
a small gravel road, and continue on the trail as it curves toward the river
and comes to a wooden bridge across the Roaring Fork River. After
crossing the bridge, stay right for about 100 feet along the other side of
the river and up a bank. You will emerge onto a broad brush flat with
scrub oak—the old river terrace and site of part of the old stage route
between Aspen and Independence—where the trail levels off until it
enters the trees and comes to Difficult Creek about one-half mile into the
hike. Here you enter the Wilderness as the route rises through a pine and
fir forest, at first along Difficult Creek, and then turning away from it.
Almost 2 miles into the hike the trail dips through a gully with a small
creek flowing through it. Beyond this, the trail enters a rocky area and
starts ascending quite steeply. Here it is possible to catch occasional
good views toward both Aspen and Independence Pass.

About 2½ miles into the hike the trail levels off in the forest of pine, spruce, and aspen, and again picks up the roaring, bouldered Difficult Creek, which it follows the rest of the way. A little further on are the remains of four cabins in the forest before the trail starts ascending again. At about 3 miles the sign "Trail not maintained beyond this point" indicates a good turnaround point. However, you can continue a little further (take the left fork at the sign) through the woods. You will rejoin a beautiful stretch of river where the water wildly tumbles over the boulders, but the unmaintained trail becomes covered with boulders and fallen trees, forcing you to turn back.

A beautiful stand of aspen along the Difficult Trail.

2. Weller Lake

Start/Finish: Weller Lake Parking Lot (9,380 feet; 13S0351135E, 4331500N)
Destination: Weller Lake (9,560 feet; 13S0351244E, 4331106N)
Round Trip: 1¼ miles / 1 hour
Difficulty: Easy
Elevation Range: 9,380–9,560 feet
Maps: USGS New York Peak; TI #127
Wilderness Designation: Collegiate Peaks Wilderness

General Comments: This fairly short and easy trail accesses a lake surrounded by spruce and aspen with rocky, barren peaks as a backdrop. The trail climbs through a lush forest, partly following the roaring outlet stream of the lake. Although the trail ends at the lake, if you enjoy scrambling over boulders and rocks you can explore along the shoreline. An optional short walk branching off from this trail takes you to a beautiful overlook of the cascading Roaring Fork River.

Directions to Trailhead: Drive east from Aspen on Highway 82 about 8 miles (.3 mile past mile marker 49) to a parking pullout on the right just before Weller Campground.

Trail Route: Follow the marked trail out of the far end of the parking area through the aspen and along the Roaring Fork River to a bridge (two minutes from the parking area). Cross the bridge and go up the steps in the bank to an immediate fork, where you will go to the right. (Going to the left will take you to the Roaring Fork Overlook.) You will soon see a sign showing that you are entering the Collegiate Peaks Wilderness. Continue to climb through the lush, bouldered forest of evergreens and aspen via a series of switchbacks. After you cross a small bridge over the Weller Lake outlet stream, it is only another five minutes to the north end of the lake,

Taking a rest at Weller Lake.

where the trail ends. On the way back, if you have time, take the fork to the Roaring Fork Overlook. This side trail leads through the forest along the river for a little over ¼ mile to the overlook of the river.

3. Grottos

Start/Finish: Grottos Parking Lot (9,480 feet; 13S0352740E, 4331326N)
Destination: Scenic area along the Roaring Fork River
Round Trip: 1 hour
Difficulty: Easy
Maps: USGS New York Peak; TI #127
Wilderness Designation: Non-Wilderness

General Comments: The Grottos is really more of a picnic, exploration, and sunbathing area than a trail. Many interesting rock formations, including the "ice caves", have been carved out by the Roaring Fork River in this area. The rock cliffs rising in the background, the cascading river crashing over boulders (the Cascades), and the sculptured rocks all create an ideal setting for a picnic and some leisure time. The old stage road trail alongside the Grottos leads to the confluence of the Roaring Fork River and Lincoln Creek, and makes for a very pleasant short walk. On most good weather days, especially on weekends, this area will be quite crowded.

Directions to Trailhead: Take Highway 82 east from Aspen about 9 miles (.4 miles past the 50-mile marker and 1 mile past the Weller Campground) and turn right down a slightly rough gravel road 200 feet to the parking area. Restrooms and picnic tables are available.

Trail Route: Just before the bridge, a map of the Grottos is displayed. From the parking area cross the bridge over the Roaring Fork River and go to the left on the main trail, which was the old stagecoach route between Leadville and Aspen. Just past the bridge are "erratic boulders" left by glaciers 8,000 years ago in indents on the huge flat rocks. Just beyond the "erratic boulders" the trail is indicated going to the left. (Going straight ahead takes you on the old stage road about ¼ mile to the confluence of Lincoln Creek and the Roaring Fork River, a very pleasant walk. Alongside the old stage road a small canyon follows the path on the left.) Signs on the main trail indicate the way to the Cascades and the ice caves. These subterranean sculptured cavities, carved out of the rock by the river, contain ice most of the summer, but care must be taken in exploring, as the rocks and ice are very slippery and wet. The best place to picnic is right by the river on the large boulders by the Cascades.

Exploring the ice caves fairly late in the summer, when the ice is almost gone.

4. Braille Trail & Discovery Trail

Start/Finish: Braille Trail & Discovery Trail Parking Lot (10,310 feet; 13S0357627E, 4332006N)
Round Trip: ¼ mile / one hour
Difficulty: Very easy
Maps: USGS New York Peak; TI #127
Wilderness Designation: Non-Wilderness

General Comments: The self-guided Braille nature trail in a spruce and fir forest is designed for the blind, but is also a wonderful educational experience for children and adults. A guide wire connects 22 stations, which have texts in Braille and in print with information on the special outdoor experience at each station. Brochures about the trail and the stations are available at the beginning of the trail.

The Braille Trail was established in 1967, when it was the first of its kind anywhere in the world. The sighted can walk the trail with eyes closed or open, but probably would benefit the most by doing the trail first with eyes closed, then with eyes open.

The Discovery Trail, located adjacent to the Braille Trail, is a wheelchair accessible gravel path that leads through the forest alongside the Roaring Fork River, and has numerous stops with benches and picnic tables. The emphasis is on discovering and observing high-elevation plants and animals in this unique mountain environment. The sign at the beginning requests that you pay close attention to your surroundings. Smell, look, listen, and touch. See how the parts of this ecosystem work together.

Directions to Trailhead: Take Highway 82 southeast from Aspen for 12 miles (.8 miles past the 53-mile marker) to a gravel road and small parking circle for the trailhead on the right. A sign for the Braille Trail & Discovery Trail is posted about 1,000 feet before the turnoff.

Trail Route: The Braille Trail starts at the parking lot and follows a route over glacial moraine and through forest and meadow right near the Roaring Fork River. The distance between stations is anywhere from a few feet to over 100 feet.

Here is the description at a typical station: Station #5: "Within your reach are the branches of the Engelmann Spruce and the subalpine fir tree. The spruce needles are sharp and rigid and feel four-sided. The fir needles are flat and blunt. Both have characteristic smells. To remember

fir from spruce, think of soft as fir to the touch. These needles are shed continually all year round, but so few at a time that the trees are always green."

Other subjects discussed and experienced at the stations include the following: timber line, the Roaring Fork River, squirrels and other small mammals, the juniper bush, needles and soil, growth rings on a stump, tree bark, lichen and fungus, rotting trees, peat moss, wound in trunk of a tree caused by a porcupine, river stones, willow and birch leaves, lodgepole pine, and plant life. After completing a fairly level loop, the trail ends up back at the parking lot, where you can then walk along the Discovery Trail.

The Discovery Trail's stops focus on the river, wildlife, the trees, and the zones (alpine, tundra, subalpine, montane, valley floor).

5. New York Creek Trail

Start/Finish: New York Creek Trailhead (10,110 feet; 13S0356462E, 4328538N)
Destination: New York Creek Pass (12,290 feet; 13S0353359E, 4324311N)
Round Trip: 8 miles / 5–6 hours
Difficulty: Moderate/difficult
Elevation Range: 10,110–12,290 feet
Maps: USGS New York Peak; TI #127
Wilderness Designation: Collegiate Peaks Wilderness

General Comments: This trail passes through spruce and fir forests, meadows with wildflowers, following New York Creek to a beautiful high alpine meadow above timber line, and ending at a 12,290-foot pass on a ridge which acts as the boundary separating the White River National Forest from the Gunnison National Forest. The views from the pass of the surrounding mountains are magnificent. Wildflowers are usually abundant in the high alpine meadow. Extended hikes above timber line may also be taken from the pass.

The ride to the trailhead along the scenic, bouldered Lincoln Creek adds to the beauty of this trip. Many people take the extra time to picnic or explore along the creek. There are also a number of designated campsites along Lincoln Creek Road.

Directions to Trailhead: Take Highway 82 east from Aspen 10 miles (just past mile marker 51) to Lincoln Creek Road on the right, go 3.3 miles up the somewhat bumpy but scenic Lincoln Creek Road to the trailhead parking on the right.

Trail Route: To start this hike you have to make your way from the parking area straight across Lincoln Creek, which tends to spread out over a large area, especially during the early part of the summer. Log bridges should be there to make the crossing easier. Basically, you will be following an old jeep road through the stream bed area. After clearing the water, pick up the old road heading uphill from the creek. Continue on the old road through an evergreen forest for almost a mile, where you will come to a clearing. Follow the trail uphill for a hundred yards or so to meet with the old aqueduct road. (Make note of this intersection for your return trip—it is not marked, and is very easily missed if you are not looking for it.) New York Peak can be seen ahead on the right at this point.

Follow the level aqueduct road to the right for a little over one-quarter mile to the first creek diversion at Brooklyn Gulch. Continue on the road around the corner for about 3-4 more minutes and watch for a trail going into the woods on the left (with a sign "New York Trail #2182" where the trail enters the woods). If you miss the turnoff and reach the end of the road at the New York Creek Diversion, backtrack for a couple of hundred feet to the trail. Follow this trail up through a beautiful evergreen forest as it parallels New York Creek for three-quarters mile to a stream crossing, which brings you into the open valley. After another mile of climbing through meadows and patches of fir and spruce, the trail bends to the west and climbs steeply through trees along a stream for a half mile, until, after one last steep switchback, it emerges into the beautiful Upper Meadows. From this point rock cairns and wooden posts mark the trail as it heads through the marshy and sometimes snowy tundra to the pass on the ridge ahead.

6. Grizzly Lake

Start/Finish: Grizzly Lake Trailhead (10,630 feet; 13S0360598E, 4326587N)
Destination: Grizzly Lake (12,515 feet; 13S0362147E, 4323697N)
Round Trip: 7½ miles / 4–6 hours
Difficulty: Moderate/difficult (steep sections and high altitude)
Elevation Range: 10,630–12,515 feet
Maps: USGS Independence Pass; TI #127
Wilderness Designation: Collegiate Peaks Wilderness

General Comments: The Grizzly Lake Trail takes you through a valley along the Continental Divide, up to a deep alpine lake located above timber line at 12,515 feet elevation at the base of 13,988-foot Grizzly Peak. Rocky Mountain goats can frequently be seen on the rocky Continental Divide ridge above the lake. The lake will usually still be frozen early in the summer because of the high elevation, and you may have to wade the one stream crossing early in the summer during runoff. Wildflowers abound along the route in the latter part of the summer. The lake is partially surrounded by a number of rock slides extending right into the lake from the rocky semicircle of peaks, so care should be exercised when exploring along the shoreline. Get an early start, since thunderstorms are very common and dangerous in the afternoons at this high elevation.

Grizzly Creek and Grizzly Peak as seen from the Continental Divide.

Directions to Trailhead: Take Highway 82 east from Aspen 10 miles (just past mile marker 51) to Lincoln Creek Road on the right, go 6.3 miles up this road (a slow, bumpy, but scenic drive along Lincoln Creek) to Grizzly Reservoir, and then stay left a tenth of a mile toward the campground to the trailhead on the left.

The trailhead is located in the trees directly opposite several buildings by the reservoir. Just before and after the trailhead are a few spots to park. If you enter the campground, you've gone too far.

Trail Route: The first one-half mile is a climb through spruce and fir trees up switchbacks, accompanied by the roar of Grizzly Creek. As the trail emerges from the dense tree cover, it levels off somewhat and gently ascends on the left (north) side of Grizzly Creek through an open stream valley dotted with spruce trees, and surrounded by rocky, barren peaks.

At 2 miles the trail passes through the fourth and last grove of spruce, where you will see the remains of an old log cabin, and exits into a field of wildflowers. The trail continues down to cross Grizzly Creek, and starts heading uphill as the entire valley bends to the right, as if to avoid the Continental Divide ahead.

As the route gets steeper, the trail works its way around and up a rocky cliff area toward a shelf with a year-round snow cornice in the background. The last three-quarters mile consists of ascending this rocky shelf area, including passing through a couple of small marshy areas. Just after passing a pond you reach one last long uphill traversing switchback that brings you to Grizzly Lake on the left (which you won't see until you're right on top of it) at the foot of Grizzly Peak. Earlier in the summer much of this final portion may be snow-covered.

7. Anderson & Petroleum Lakes

Start/Finish: Petroleum Lake Trailhead (11,280 feet; 13S0360015E, 4321291N)
Destination: Petroleum Lake (12,315 feet; 13S0358419E, 4321072N)
Round Trip: 4 miles / 3 hours
Difficulty: Easy/moderate (but the driving to the trailhead is difficult)
Elevation Range: 11,280–12,315 feet
Maps: USGS New York Peak, Independence Pass; TI #127
Wilderness Designation: Non-Wilderness

General Comments: Anderson and Petroleum Lakes are located a mile apart from each other above timber line in the tundra, surrounded by rocky knolls and peaks. They are situated in one of the most picturesque settings accessible from the Lincoln Creek Valley. The hike through the woods, meadows, and tundra abounds with wildflowers, and the drive to the trailhead is almost as picturesque as the hike. The Lincoln Creek

Road follows a cascading stream to Grizzly Reservoir, beyond which the road passes through a beautiful mountain valley. Past the reservoir the road can only be driven by high clearance four-wheel drive vehicles. All others will have to park and hike (or bike) from the Portal Campground by Grizzly Reservoir, which adds about 6 miles to the round trip.

Directions to Trailhead: Take Highway 82 southeast from Aspen 10 miles (just past mile marker 51) to Lincoln Creek Road on the right, drive up this somewhat bumpy road for 6.3 miles to Grizzly Reservoir, and to the Portal Campground beyond. Go straight past the campground and continue on the 4-wheel drive rough road through the gate. High clearance is required. Three miles from the campground, 10 miles from when you first turned onto Lincoln Creek Road, you will come to a main fork in the road (.4 mile beyond an old cabin on the left side of the road). Take this right, go across the creek, and park on the other side.

Petroleum Lake surrounded by 13,500-foot peaks.

Trail Route: The entire route follows an old mining road, so it's hard to lose the way. The trail passes an old cabin on the right and climbs through the fir to the right of Anderson Creek. Two separate gates block the way to vehicles. At about one-half mile into the hike, still accompanied by the cascading creek, you will start seeing the rocky peaks jutting up ahead. After passing the ruins of a couple of cabins, the trail enters the tundra and soon forks to the left to Anderson Lake, which sits in a little basin against the rocky backdrop.

To get to Petroleum Lake, follow the right fork of the jeep road as it goes up through the tundra and wildflowers, contours around the rock faces off to the left, and stays left of the prominent Larson Peak. After passing to the left of a large pond, you will see the outlet stream tumbling down from Petroleum Lake. Stay on the steep path to the right of the stream to get to the lake. If you have extra time, try exploring the area beyond the lake with its interesting rocky knolls, little basins, and overlooks.

8. Midway Pass

Start/Finish: Lost Man Trailhead (10,520 feet; 13S0359601E, 4331569N)
Destination: Midway Pass (11,865 feet; 13S0356918E, 4334743N)
Round Trip: 7 miles / 4–5 hours
Difficulty: Moderate/difficult (initial steepness, and trail-finding difficulty early in the season)
Elevation Range: 10,520–12,155 feet
Maps: USGS Independence Pass, Mt. Champion, Thimble Rock; TI #127
Wilderness Designation: Hunter–Fryingpan Wilderness

General Comments: Midway Pass is a wonderful destination that gets the hiker into the alpine tundra for unsurpassed views of the Elk Mountains, Williams Mountains, and the Continental Divide. The switchbacking ascent to the alpine tundra through lodgepole pine and spruce takes you through one of the most beautiful forests east of aspen. A variety of wildlife can also be encountered in this high country area. The upper part of the trail can be hard to follow at times, especially early in the summer when snow is still present in the high, marshy meadows.

Directions to Trailhead: Take Highway 82 east from Aspen 14 miles to the parking lot on the left across from Lost Man Campground (just past mile marker 55).

Trail Route: The trail goes left (west) from the parking lot and crosses a small bridge. Stay left at the first trail fork, and one-quarter mile past the bridge take the Midway Trail (should be marked by a sign) going left up the hill. The trail makes 18 switchbacks up through the lodgepole pine, giving you good views toward Independence Pass.

After gaining about 1,000 feet in elevation in a mile, you will reach the top of the switchbacks as the trail enters the Hunter–Fryingpan Wilderness. Here you ascend gradually through spruce, as the route starts opening up into the quiet beauty of the higher elevations. Soon you can see rock walls ahead to the right, beyond which the Williams Mountains lie. In front of you are scrub willows and marshy meadows, which have to be crossed to get to the pass. Mountain peaks are evident in every direction.

After crossing the marshy (or snowy) area, the trail continues to the right up a rounded, undulating ridge, and stays along the right side of the Coleman Creek drainage, passing to the right of a small pond—a great lunch spot. After reaching the high point on the shoulder of a ridge, the trail takes a gradual descending traverse to the left toward the low point in the gap ahead. The low point in this gap is Midway Pass, your destination, generally unmarked by any signs.

9. Linkins Lake

Start/Finish: Linkins Lake Trailhead (11,505 feet; 13S0363274E, 4331798N)
Destination: Linkins Lake (12,015 feet; 13S0362759E, 43332188N)
Round Trip: 1¼ miles / 1 hour
Difficulty: Moderate (high altitude and steepness)
Elevation Range: 11,505–12,015 feet
Maps: USGS Mt. Champion, Independence Pass; TI #127
Wilderness Designation: Hunter–Fryingpan Wilderness

General Comments: Linkins Lake is located near Independence Pass in a small glacial cirque at an elevation of 12,015 feet. This high alpine lake commands good views of peaks on the Continental Divide. The entire hike to Linkins Lake is above timber line, and passes through tundra containing a wide variety of alpine flowers which bloom in the latter part of the summer. Because of the late snowmelt at this high altitude, it's best to wait at least until early/mid July before hiking this trail. Start early in the day, as thunderstorms can move in quickly in the early afternoon.

Directions to Trailhead: Take Highway 82 east from Aspen about 18 miles (.2 mile past mile marker 59) to the parking area for the trailhead on the left at a hairpin turn in the road. The ghost town of Independence on the right at mile marker 57 (a little over 2 miles before the trailhead) makes a pleasant historical stop on the way.

Trail Route: From the trailhead at the parking area, the Linkins Lake Trail and the Lost Man Trail ascend together for about 200 yards. Just after a stream crossing, at the Hunter–Fryingpan Wilderness sign, the Lost Man Trail forks off to the right and the Linkins Lake Trail goes left. From this point the

Linkins Lake/Lost Man Loop fork.

Linkins Lake Trail climbs fairly steeply through scrub willow and wildflowers toward the bench on the left, where the glacial cirque containing the lake is located. The trail levels off in the tundra as it makes the final approach to the lake.

10. Lost Man Loop

Start: Linkins Lake Trailhead (11,505 feet; 13S0363274E, 4331798N)
Finish: Lost Man Trailhead (10,520 feet; 13S0359601E, 4331569N)
Round Trip: 8½ miles / 5–7 hours
Difficulty: Moderate/difficult (high altitude, some steepness and rough sections of trail)
Elevation Range: 10,520–12,815 feet
Maps: USGS Mt. Champion, Independence Pass, New York Peak; TI #127
Wilderness Designation: Hunter–Fryingpan Wilderness

General Comments: The Lost Man Loop is a high altitude scenic hike beginning near Independence Pass. The trail takes you up through an area shaped by glaciers just below the rocky ridge of the Continental Divide, through tundra and a multitude of wildflowers, along the upper Roaring Fork River to its source (Independence Lake). It then crosses a 12,815-foot pass to Lost Man Lake. From there it follows Lost Man Creek down from its source (Lost Man Lake). Below timber line the second half of the route passes through incredible stands of spruce and more wildflowers as it heads toward Lost Man Reservoir. Due to snowmelt, many portions of the trail are marshy and wet; the trail is driest in August and September. Even though snow and marshy sections may obscure parts of the trail, it would be hard to get lost since you are following two stream valleys. It is not uncommon to see ptarmigan in the rocks at the high point of the route above the lakes.

This trail is not a real "loop", as it starts 4 miles up the road from where it ends, so an extra drop-off car can make getting back to the starting point easier. The loop is best hiked in the direction described here, so that the high altitude area can be cleared before the traditional afternoon thundershowers. It also is more of a downhill hike when the loop is done counterclockwise.

Directions to Trailhead: Take Highway 82 east from Aspen about 14 miles (just beyond mile marker 55) to where a parking lot on the left, directly across from Lost Man Campground, marks the finish of this loop. This is where a second car can be dropped off, or you can park and catch a ride up the road to the start of the loop. Continue on Highway 82 a little over two miles beyond the ghost town of Independence to a hairpin turn one-quarter mile past mile marker 59 (18 miles east of Aspen), where a parking area on the left marks the start of the trail. This is also the trailhead for the Linkins Lake Trail.

Trail Route: Follow the trail for about 5 minutes to where it forks at the Wilderness boundary just across the stream coming down from Linkins Lake. Take the right fork for the Lost Man Trail (left goes to Linkins Lake), and continue along the left side of the Roaring Fork River for a quarter mile to where the trail crosses to the other side. After following the east side of the stream for over one-half mile, the trail comes to a large marshy bowl and heads up to the right onto a plateau above the bowl. During the earlier part of the summer the trail may be marshy and snow-covered, but later it is quite well-defined.

At 1¾ miles the trail crosses the Roaring Fork (outlet stream) in the rocks just below Independence Lake (12,490 feet), and follows the west (left) side of the lake, taking you up to a large saddle (12,815 feet; 13S0364610E, 4334407N) which separates the Roaring Fork drainage from the Lost Man drainage. From the pass you have spectacular views of the surrounding mountain ranges. On the right is the Continental Divide, and just below is the rock-encircled Lost Man Lake, one of the most scenic settings in the area.

As you descend toward the 12,450-foot lake from the saddle, keep an eye out for ptarmigan amongst the rocks. Stay along the right side of the lake; at the far end of the lake the trail bears to the right of the outlet stream. The trail continues down to the right around the rock promontory in front of you, and gradually curves around from the right into the beautiful Lost Man basin.

As the trail descends toward the swampy valley below, it swings back to the left of the large rounded rock which divides the upper part of the valley in two, and gradually descends toward the marshy valley floor, bearing to the right as the creek becomes better defined. This section may have some muddy spots earlier in the year, as the trail works its way through the scrub growth.

About 1½ miles from the lake, as the creek starts turning to the left (southwest), the trail goes straight, gradually ascending over a broad ridge, and then starts dropping toward the entrance to Deadman Gulch on the right. When you come to the "T" in the trail (the well-signed junction with the trail to South Fork Pass), go left on the Lost Man Trail to continue down the valley formed by Lost Man Creek. You will descend back to the creek and remain on the right side of the valley for the rest of the hike.

About 2 miles from the "T" you will cross Jack Creek on a large log in a beautiful wooded area. Within a mile you will be in the large open meadow, with Lost Man Reservoir at the far end. Stay on the trail along the right side of the reservoir, and 100 yards past the reservoir stay straight on a shortcut as the trail splits (going right up a little hill takes you past the intersection with the Midway Trail—a little longer route; however, the shortcut trail may be closed off). After several hundred yards you will rejoin the main trail and then cross a wooden bridge, where you can see the parking lot across from Lost Man Campground just ahead. At the parking lot you are now 4 miles down Highway 82 from where you started, and will have to catch a ride up the road to your car if you have not dropped a car here.

11. Continental Divide

Start/Finish: Independence Pass Parking Lot (12,110 feet; 13S0364758E, 4329964N)
Destination: Peak 13,045 (13,045 feet; 13S0362956E, 4327238N)
Round Trip: 4 miles / 3–4 hours
Difficulty: Moderate (high altitude and steady climb)
Elevation Range: 12,110–13,045 feet
Maps: USGS Independence Pass; TI #127
Wilderness Designation: Collegiate Peaks Wilderness

General Comments: The Continental Divide is a string of summits of Rocky Mountain peaks that separates the streams flowing toward the Gulf of California and the Pacific Ocean to the west, from those flowing toward the Gulf of Mexico and the Atlantic Ocean to the east. This particular route on the Continental Divide offers the hiker with a limited amount of time or experience the opportunity to hike to over 13,000 feet, and see a number of the 14,000-foot peaks of Central Colorado. Access to the trailhead is by a paved highway that winds up to the Divide from Aspen (to the west), and from Twin Lakes and Leadville (to the east); this drive alone is an adventure.

The hiker should realize that the entire hike is over 12,000 feet and oxygen is quite sparse, so be prepared to go slowly. It is best to do the hike early in the day—afternoon thunderstorms are common at this elevation. The ridge is wide enough to be easy to hike, but some of the drop-offs along the latter part of the trail might affect those with a fear of heights. Great care should also be taken to stay on the trail, so as not to impact the very fragile tundra. Alpine tundra wildflowers are abundant along the ridge. Be sure to bring extra clothes to protect you from the cold, wind, and rain that you may encounter.

Directions to Trailhead: The Independence Pass parking lot is located on Highway 82, about 20 miles east of Aspen, .2 mile past the 61-mile marker, right on the Continental Divide. From Leadville, take Highway 24 south to Highway 82, which you will then take west through Twin Lakes to Independence Pass, a total distance of about 40 miles.

Trail Route: From the parking lot at Independence Pass you can see the Continental Divide ridge extending to the west and south. About 100 yards up the paved path from the parking lot, follow the gravel old jeep trail on the right leading toward the ridge. During this gradual ascent, off to the west you will begin to see the 14,000-foot peaks of the Elk Mountain Range. After almost a mile you will be starting your climb up the ridge toward the first peak, Peak 12,812. Another 20–25 minutes of steady climbing will get you to the nice flat area on top of the first peak.

From here the trail descends a little before climbing to the next peak, Peak 13,045, which is your goal. Both sides of the trail, especially the left, are marked by steep drop-offs. The ghost town of Independence can be seen in the distance down to the right. Soon the ridge becomes very rocky, as you ascend the last section along the right side of the ridge. The summit of Peak 13,045 is marked by a small rock shelter and a rock monument. Grizzly Peak (13,988 feet) looms ahead; the Grizzly Creek Valley is to the south, and the Lincoln Creek Valley lies off to the west. Take time to look around—often you can see a herd of Rocky Mountain goats grazing on the flanks of the next peak on the divide, Peak 13,198. Return via the same route.

The ridge of the Continental Divide, the route of this hike.

Aspen

Aspen, the former silver mining town, is now a haven for culture and outdoor activities. During the summer, hiking tops the list of how to enjoy the scenic wonders of one of the most beautiful areas in the country. There is virtually no end to the number of different hiking routes available at this outdoors Mecca.

Hikes #12–17 are all accessible from Aspen by foot or local bus. They range in steepness from the virtually flat Rio Grande Trail (#12), to the almost vertical Ute Trail (#13). The other four explore Red and Smuggler mountains and the hanging valley, Hunter Valley, located between these two mountains, which rise above Aspen to the north and east.

Hikes #18 and #19 are both reached by the road that accesses the ghost town of Ashcroft. These two popular hikes, which start near Ashcroft, lead to mountain lakes at timber line ringed by rocky peaks.

Hikes #20–22 start at Maroon Lake, at the foot of the Maroon Bells, probably the most photographed setting in the continental United States. Both Buckskin Pass (#21) and West Maroon Pass (#22) are long, rigorous hikes that lead to spectacular views of the surrounding mountains.

12. Rio Grande Trail

Start/Finish: Herron Park (7,920 feet; 13S0343386E, 4339392N)
Puppy Smith by Post Office (7,900 feet; 13S0342894E, 4339912N)
Stein Park by Cemetery Lane (7,735 feet; 13S0341123E, 4341872N)
One-Way Distances from Herron Park: (Puppy Smith) .6 miles; (Stein Park) 2.4 miles; (Open valley) 4.5 miles
Difficulty: Easy
Elevation Range: (Open valley) 7,600 feet – (Aspen) 7,920 feet
Maps: USGS Aspen; TI #127
Wilderness Designation: Non-Wilderness

General Comments: The Rio Grande Trail is easily accessible on foot from the center of Aspen, and is popular with walkers, hikers, runners, bicyclists, and, in the winter, cross-country skiers. It provides an easy, scenic route along the Roaring Fork River on the old Denver and Rio Grande Railroad bed in Aspen, with the option of continuing on the trail west of Cemetery Lane toward Woody Creek and Basalt. The portion from Herron Park (east end of Aspen) to Cemetery Lane (west end of Aspen) is paved. West of Cemetery Lane the trail is gravel to Woody Creek, beyond which the trail is paved to Basalt. The first mile of the trail west of Cemetery Lane offers some scenic spots to enjoy the Roaring Fork River and picnic or fish. Beyond that, the trail continues high above the Roaring Fork River in the open valley.

Directions to Trailheads: (Herron Park) Walk east on Main Street (Highway 82) in Aspen to the curve at Original Street and take an immediate left on Neale Street; go over No Problem Bridge to Herron Park on the left just beyond the bridge.

(Puppy Smith) Walk north on Mill Street past the Hotel Jerome (at Main Street) and take the second street (Puppy Smith Street) to the left toward the post office. Just beyond the post office on the right are the signs for the Rio Grande Trail, as the concrete trail heads off to the right.

(Stein Park) Take Highway 82 (Main Street) west out of Aspen across the Castle Creek bridge to the first light (Cemetery Lane) and turn right. Just over one mile down the road, on the other side of the bridge (Slaughterhouse Bridge) over the Roaring Fork River, is the parking lot on the left for Stein Park. You can also take the Snowbunny Bus from town to Red Butte Drive just before the bridge and walk the last 100 yards.

Trail Route: (From Herron Park) The trail leaves the park and immediately crosses a bridge over the Roaring Fork River, which it follows on the left side, until a trail intersection takes you to the right across an old bridge to the Aspen Art Museum. Just past the museum you pass under Mill Street and hook up with the trail coming from the post office at .6 miles from Herron Park.

(From Puppy Smith) The trail passes over bridges spanning the Roaring Fork River and Hunter Creek and continues along the north side of the Roaring Fork River. A 1½-mile measured course is indicated by signs along the route. At 1.8 miles from the starting point, the trail crosses under Cemetery Lane at the Slaughterhouse Bridge and enters Stein Park.

(From Stein Park) The smooth gravel path signed as the Rio Grande Trail heads west along the right side of the Roaring Fork River from Stein Park. In the first mile you follow a beautiful stretch of the bouldered, rushing Roaring Fork River, bordered by steep rocky walls on the other side. At ¼ mile from the park the trail passes under a rocky overhang, which still has signs of smoke visible from the trains coming into Aspen during the mining era of the late nineteenth century. At .6 miles you pass a large beautiful pond on your right. At one mile a side trail, the Stein Trail, goes down to the left, over a bridge across the river, and up the steep bank on the other side to the Aspen Business Center. At 1.3 miles water pours down from the rocks above on your right. At 1.5 miles you are directly across from the Aspen Metro Sanitation District facility, as the trail gets more into the open, high above the Roaring Fork River. As the trail emerges into the open valley, with views of Brush Creek, Triangle Peak, and the midvalley, any spot is good for turning around. Continuing straight takes you to Woody Creek and Basalt.

13. Ute Trail

Start/Finish: Ute Trailhead (8,020 feet; 13S0343493E, 4338467N)
Destination: Overlook (9,185 feet; 13S0343132E, 4338113N)
Round Trip: 2½ miles / 2 hours
Difficulty: Difficult (extremely steep with poor footing)
Elevation Range: 8,020–9,185 feet
Maps: USGS Aspen; TI #127
Wilderness Designation: Non-Wilderness

General Comments: The very steep, rocky Ute Trail can be reached on foot from the center of Aspen, and offers one of the best views of Aspen and the Roaring Fork Valley of any of the trails in the area. Situated on Aspen Mountain to the east of the Silver Queen Gondola, the Ute Trail ends at a rock outcropping near the ski slopes, just below Gentlemen's Ridge. The climb is very steep (the trail ascends almost 1,200 feet in a little over one mile), but the view from the rocks is well worth it. The hike up this trail is a popular workout for local athletes.

Trailhead for the Ute Trail.

Directions to Trailhead: Take Main Street in Aspen (or any other east-west street south of Main Street) east to Original Street and turn right toward Aspen Mountain. Follow Original Street to the end, where you turn left onto Ute Ave. Go exactly .4 mile to the trailhead on the right, directly across from a small parking lot (about 100 feet before the entrance to Benedict Building parking). The trailhead starts at three steps formed by railroad ties, and is marked by a sign.

Trail Route: The trail switchbacks steeply up the mountain, at first through brush and small trees, then through a forest of aspen and evergreens. Initially you can see The Aspen Club and its tennis courts directly below, the subdivision of Mountain Valley across the valley to the right, and the east end of Aspen. Gradually more and more of Aspen is visible, until the trail ends at the rock outcropping at 9,185 feet elevation, from where Aspen, the Roaring Fork Valley, Mount Sopris (to the west), and the Independence Pass area (to the east) spread out before you. The rock formation jutting out toward the town offers a number of places to sit down and have a small picnic or lunch, although, if you have a fear of heights, you may be slightly uncomfortable.

14. Smuggler Mountain

Start/Finish: Parking at Smuggler Mountain Road (8,010 feet; 3S0343833E, 4339599N)
Destination: Smuggler Mountain "Platform" (8,835 feet; 13S0344173E, 4340486N)
Round Trip: 3 miles / 1–2 hours
Difficulty: Moderate (steepness)
Elevation Range: 8,010–8,835 feet
Maps: USGS Aspen; TI #127
Wilderness Designation: Non-Wilderness

General Comments: Although this is a jeep road and not a trail, this route is included because it is one of Aspen's most accessible and most popular routes. For those who want a quick, yet good, workout that provides some of the best views of Aspen, this is the hike. The trail climbs about 800 feet in elevation past the Smuggler Mine and some other old mine sites to a viewpoint known as the "Platform", because of the wooden platform on the ground there. The road is fairly steep, and is also used by bikers and an occasional vehicle. The trailhead can easily be reached by foot from downtown Aspen.

The view of Aspen from the "Platform" on Smuggler Mountain.

Directions to Trailhead: Go north on Mill Street from the Hotel Jerome, cross the river, turn right on Gibson, and go up a short steep hill. At the top bear left on Park Circle, staying on the right of the blue-roofed Centennial Condominiums. In a quarter mile, just past the condominiums, Smuggler Mountain Road switchbacks up the side of the mountain on the left. There is parking both on Park Circle and on Smuggler Mountain Road.

Trail Route: Start on the switchbacks, staying to the right of the Smuggler Mine at the beginning. Be aware of the private driveways during the first part of the route. Continue on the long, steady climb up the side of Smuggler Mountain until you eventually round a curve and head into the woods on your right. The "Platform", the usual destination, will be on your right up a short, steep bank. Take the time to enjoy the views of Aspen and the Roaring Fork Valley. You can add to the workout by continuing up to the right, on Smuggler Mountain Road, for up to another 4 miles through the woods. Parts of this section are quite steep, and other parts traverse gently through the woods. The road eventually ends at Warren Lakes, about 6 miles from the trailhead.

15. Hunter Valley

Start/Finish: Hunter Creek Trail Parking Lot (8,280 feet; 13S0343495E, 4340667N)
Destination: Hunter Valley (9,000 feet; 13S0349362E, 4341096N)
Round Trip: 3–7 miles / 2–4 hours
Difficulty: Easy/moderate (some steepness at beginning)
Elevation Range: 8,270–9,000 feet
Maps: USGS Aspen, Thimble Rock; TI #127
Wilderness Designation: Non-Wilderness

General Comments: This hike offers a closer access to Hunter Valley than the Hunter Creek–Smuggler Loop (#16), but doesn't cover the beautiful, lower part of the bouldered Hunter Creek from the Hunter Creek Condominiums, although it could also be started from that point. The Hunter Valley meadows, with their wildflowers and abandoned cabins, the abundant wildlife, and the scenic views of the mountains, make this popular for a relatively short hike and picnic. It's not necessary to do the full seven miles to enjoy this hike—you can turn around anywhere, even to the point of getting in a good 3-mile hike. Be aware that this trail is often used by mountain bikers, so be ready to step to the side when you hear or see a biker approaching.

Directions to Trailhead: Take Mill Street north from Main Street (by Hotel Jerome). After crossing the bridge over the Roaring Fork, bear left onto Red Mountain Road and follow to Hunter Creek Road (1.4 miles from Main Street with a sign for Hunter Creek Trail Parking Lot). Go right for one-quarter mile, then left into the Hunter Creek Trail Parking Lot. Trail access is by the brown building, where the road turns into the parking lot. (Note: This trail can also be accessed by the trailhead for the Hunter Creek–Smuggler Loop).

Trail Route: The trail ascends a small ridge above the parking lot through scrub oak, drops through a gully, again goes up bearing to the right onto a driveway, then across Hunter Creek Road to a gravel trail marked Hunter Creek Trail, and traverses the side of a hill to the Benedict Bridge. At this point Hunter Creek is separating Red Mountain on the left from Smuggler Mountain on the right.

After the bridge, the trail ascends on an old jeep road along the roaring Hunter Creek through aspen, spruce, and pine. At about one-half mile, when it crosses a private road, stay straight up the hill on the trail into the aspen. In a couple hundred yards the trail enters Forest Service land, as a large meadow and Hunter Valley open up ahead. In the meadow, about 200 yards past the Forest Service sign, a trail forks up to the right (stay straight). In another 200 yards take a left across the Tenth Mountain Bridge, and continue along the other side of the creek in the meadow on an old jeep road which passes some old cabins. Stay right at a trail fork, and continue along Hunter Creek until you come to a wooden bridge ("reservoir bridge") on the right crossing the creek. (Note this bridge; you can use it for the return trip on the other side of the creek.) Continue straight on the trail along the north side of Hunter Creek. This portion of the trail has many good picnic spots, plus good views up and down the valley. Up the valley the Williams Mountains are visible, and eventually a large rock known as Thimble Rock can be seen. Remains of several old cabins are located in the meadows along the route. After almost two miles, where the valley has narrowed up and the trail comes in closer contact with the creek, the trail becomes obliterated by fallen trees, brush, water, etc., and you will have to retrace your route back to Aspen.

16. Hunter Creek–Smuggler Loop

Start/Finish: Hunter Creek Trailhead by Hunter Creek Condominiums (7,895 feet; 13S0343166E, 4340047N)
Destination: Hunter Valley and Smuggler Mountain
Round Trip: 6 miles / 3–4 hours
Difficulty: Moderate (some steeper parts with poor footing, otherwise mostly easy)
Elevation Range: 7,895–9,010 feet
Maps: USGS Aspen; TI #127
Wilderness Designation: Non-Wilderness

General Comments: Hunter Valley, located between Smuggler Mountain and Red Mountain, is a hanging valley that is very popular with hikers and bikers in the summer, and cross-country skiers and snowshoers in the winter. The trail begins and ends in Aspen, and the trailhead is easily accessible by foot or bus. The hike covers a variety of sights, including the roaring, boulder-filled Hunter Creek, the meadows of Hunter Valley with its abundant wildlife, views of the Elk Mountains, and a trip down Smuggler Mountain with great views of the town of Aspen. Except for the lower part of the trail below the Benedict Bridge, which is steep and rocky, the loop is often used by mountain bikers, so be ready to step to the side when you hear or see a biker approaching. In late spring and early summer, when the water is high, the lower part of the trail can sometimes have water over it, in which case it would be better to start at the upper trailhead as described under "Hunter Valley" (#15). The loop can also be shortened to 4½ miles (see narrative).

Directions to Trailhead: By foot or by car: go north on Mill Street from Main Street (by Hotel Jerome), cross the bridge over the Roaring Fork, bear left on Red Mountain Road, then take the next right onto Lone Pine Road. The trailhead is about 100 yards on the left by the Hunter Creek Condominiums (one-half mile from the center of town). By bus: take the Hunter Creek Bus and get off at the Hunter Creek Condominiums.

The Hunter Creek Trailhead.

Trail Route: The trail descends down a path with wood railings to Hunter Creek, which it follows, going over walkways, through aspen, willows, scrub oak, and crossing Hunter Creek four times over bridges. The steady roar of the creek, as it passes over large boulders, accompanies you during this section of the hike, and adds an air of excitement, especially in the late spring when the water is high. Just past the second bridge over Hunter Creek, stay left at the intersection with the Lani White Trail (which can be taken back to Spruce Street by the Centennial Condominiums). The trail continues to ascend steadily with the creek, over and around rocks, until it crosses the Benedict Bridge at about one mile and enters private property, so be sure not to stray from the trail. At this point Hunter Creek is separating Red Mountain on the left from Smuggler Mountain on the right.

The trail ascends on an old jeep road along the roaring creek through aspen, spruce, and pine. After about one-half mile from the Benedict Bridge, when the trail crosses a private road, stay straight up the hill on the trail into the aspen. In another couple hundred yards the trail enters

Forest Service land as Hunter Valley opens up ahead. In the meadow, about 200 yards past the Forest Service sign, a trail forks up to the right. This trail can be taken as a shortcut to Smuggler Mountain, and will cut off about 1½ miles from this loop. Staying straight on the Hunter Valley Trail takes you past a trail on the left going across the Tenth Mountain Bridge. Continue straight along the right (south) side of Hunter Creek. (As an option, you can cross this bridge and continue along the other side of the creek in the meadow on an old jeep road, which passes some old cabins and leads to the "reservoir bridge").

In about 25 minutes after entering the meadow, you'll come to a wooden bridge ("reservoir bridge") on the left, a cabin straight ahead with a path leading to it, and a jeep road going to the right. Take a sharp right on the old jeep road, which you will be following through the aspen and more meadows on the southern edge of Hunter Valley. (You will pass the trail for the previously mentioned shortcut, which has a sign pointing straight ahead to Smuggler Mountain Road). After about three-quarters of a mile from the bridge, the road enters some pine trees and heads uphill through the forest on the back side of Smuggler Mountain. A couple of switchbacks take you past an old mining operation and a metal gate. Stay straight on the road heading uphill after the gate.

In five minutes you will come to the top of the climb at a large old mining operation, the Iowa Shaft, with its many mining tailings and an outlook over the valley. From here you gradually descend on the road through the pines for a little less than one-half mile to a road intersection and the "Platform"—an outlook over the town of Aspen from a wooden platform. This platform area is a popular destination point for bikers and hikers making the 800-foot climb up Smuggler Mountain Road from Aspen.

Continue on the road going down the side of Smuggler Mountain toward Aspen. Along here you will have dramatic views of Aspen, the Roaring Fork Valley, Mount Sopris, and the Elk Mountains as you descend toward town. Near the bottom you will pass the Smuggler Mine and come out on a paved road (Park Circle). Go right, and just past the second stop sign (Gibson), turn right on Lone Pine Road and continue past the red-roofed Hunter Creek Condominiums to the trailhead where you started.

17. Sunnyside–Hunter Valley Loop

Start: Sunnyside Trailhead at Henry Stein Park by Cemetery Lane (7,760 feet; 13S0341154E, 4341852N)
Finish: Hunter Creek Trailhead by Hunter Creek Condominiums (7,895 feet; 13S0343166E, 4340047N)
Destination: Loop through upper part of Red Mountain
Round Trip: 10 miles / 6–7 hours (not including Rio Grande Trail)
Difficulty: Moderate/difficult (steep section, routefinding)
Elevation Range: 7.760–10,100 feet
Maps: USGS Aspen; TI #127
Wilderness Designation: Non-Wilderness

General Comments: This route follows the Sunnyside Trail high along Red Mountain on the north side of Aspen, and drops into beautiful meadows in Hunter Valley on the Hunter Valley Trail. The easy accessibility of this route to Aspen, and its views of Aspen, the Roaring Fork Valley, and the Elk Mountains make it a very enjoyable local hike. The trail passes through some of the most beautiful stands of aspen trees in the Aspen area. Grouse, deer, fox, and other wildlife are frequently seen on this route. This loop is best started in the coolness of the early morning; the first part of the hike can be torment on a hot sunny day. Only the acclimated and physically fit should attempt this trail, as the first section is a steep, demanding climb. Be sure to follow the trail directions carefully; however, most ambiguous intersections are now marked by signs. Also, be aware of mountain bikers who sometimes use this route. A popular (and shorter) option is to hike up to the trees on top, take a rest and then turn around and head back down to the trailhead where you started. This option is an excellent workout for the physically fit, but it can get hot if not started early enough.

Directions to Trailhead: From downtown Aspen take the Cemetery Lane Bus to Red Butte Drive (last stop on Cemetery Lane) and walk across the bridge over the Roaring Fork River to the parking lot and Henry Stein Park on the left. If driving, go west on Highway 82 from Aspen to the first light before the golf course (Cemetery Lane), and right for 1.1 miles to a parking lot on the left, just across the Slaughterhouse Bridge. (Note: This trailhead can also be reached on foot from the center of town by taking the 1¾-mile Rio Grande paved trail to the parking lot just across Cemetery Lane.)

Trail Route: Follow the Rio Grande Trail, a nice wide path, out of the west end of the parking lot by Henry Stein Park. In less than 5 minutes, take the path going up to the right (signed Sunnyside Trail). After 7–8 minutes of climbing, you will cross McLain Flats Road and pick up the trail (signed) the other side of the road.

The Sunnyside Trail climbs up quite steeply through sagebrush, scrub oak, serviceberry, and wildflowers on Red Mountain. About a mile above the road you come to an irrigation ditch, and the trail levels off to the right along the ditch. Across the way Hayden Peak, Pyramid Peak, Mount Daly, and Mount Sopris stand out prominently. In another quarter mile the trail crosses the ditch and heads uphill, taking long switchbacks up the steep hillside for over a mile until you reach the aspen trees. In the trees you will pass some antennas, as the trail levels a little before climbing steeply again through the aspen. You will soon find yourself on a ridge, as the trail levels and a marked fork goes off to the left through the grass to the Shadyside Trail. Stay straight on the Sunnyside Trail, following a fairly level trail (with one climb thrown in) through beautiful uniform stands of aspen, with occasional great views of Aspen and the upper Roaring Fork Valley.

About one-half mile from the previous junction, you come to another intersection of Sunnyside and the Shadyside Trail (marked by a sign). Stay right on the Sunnyside Trail, which then immediately begins a narrow traverse along the south side of the mountain. You will have some good views of Aspen and the Elk Mountains to the right as the trail traverses through spruce and beautiful, tall stands of aspen. A mile past the Shadyside intersection the trail leaves the narrow traverse, and the remains of two old cabins can be seen on the right just off the trail in a grove of beautiful aspen. The trail soon starts bearing to the north as the forest changes to fir, spruce and pine.

Aspen Mountain and Aspen as seen from the Sunnyside Trail.

About one-half mile past the old cabins you will go through several small clearings and exit onto an old jeep road, which you will take a couple of hundred yards to a Y-intersection of two jeep roads (the one to the left goes to the Shadyside Trail). Go right, and stay right again when you come to a second intersection in about 150 yards. Follow the jeep road for about 15 minutes through a level forest of spruce, pine, and a few aspen. Just as the road starts to drop down to the left, the Sunnyside Trail leaves the road, heading down to the right through a few large pine trees. This intersection should be marked by a sign on the left. The trail descends down a gulch (stay right at the first immediate junction) through aspen trees to another jeep road (9,280 feet; 13S0345893E, 4342091N), where you pick up the trail on the other side of the road. (Note: The crossing jeep trail is the Hunter Creek Trail which goes left all the way to the Midway Trail and Midway Pass.)

Continue down the trail (this section is known to mountain bikers as "The Plunge") into the valley where the trail forks in the meadow just past a small water culvert under the trail. Stay right through the meadow to a jeep road, and go right on the jeep road, passing the ruins of some old hunters cabins with metal corrugated roofs. At the cabins go left onto a trail for the Tenth Mountain Bridge (sign), where you pass one more cabin remains and cross over Hunter Creek in 3–4 minutes. Go right on the trail after the bridge on the Hunter Valley Trail.

At the National Forest boundary sign the trail enters the trees and crosses an intersecting road. Continue straight ahead along the creek. In one-half mile you will cross the Benedict Bridge. Take an immediate left on the footpath descending through the trees and boulders along Hunter Creek. After a second bridge, descend steeply down some steps in the trail, and fork to the right (the Lani White Trail goes left) across another bridge. From here you will be going through some scrub growth, then will cross an irrigation ditch, Hunter Creek, and several small streams before you reach the end of the trail at the Hunter Creek Condominiums. From the condos it is only one-half mile to the center of Aspen. You can go left on the road to the bus stop, or right to Aspen or to the Rio Grande Trail.

If you have to pick up a car at the Sunnyside Trailhead, take the Hunter Creek Bus to Rubey Park, and the Cemetery Lane Bus to Red Butte Drive, and walk across the Slaughterhouse Bridge to the parking lot at Henry Stein Park. If you wish to walk the Rio Grande Trail, it is just over 2 miles to the Sunnyside Trailhead at Henry Stein Park.

18. American Lake

Start/Finish: American Lake Trailhead (9,400 feet; 13S0344235E, 4326199N)
Destination: American Lake (11,450 feet; 13S0341755E, 4324619N)
Round Trip: 6½ miles / 4 hours
Difficulty: Moderate/difficult (steepness and footing)
Elevation Range: 9,400–11,450 feet
Maps: USGS Hayden Peak; TI #127
Wilderness Designation: Maroon Bells–Snowmass Wilderness

General Comments: The trip to American Lake gives the hiker a chance to see the scenic Castle Creek Valley, the historic town of Ashcroft, and a lake nestled among rocky 12,000- and 13,000-foot peaks. The trail is almost entirely wooded and steep, climbing 2,000 feet in a little over 3 miles through beautiful groves of aspen trees and wildflower-filled meadows. This is one of the most popular lake hikes since it is a fairly short, although strenuous, hike that leads to a backcountry setting. Note that this lake is a critical cutthroat trout spawning area, especially where the trail meets the lake, so keep dogs leashed so that they don't wander into the lake and damage these spawning beds.

American Lake, still surrounded by snow in the early summer.

Directions to Trailhead: Take Highway 82 west from Aspen one-half mile to the roundabout and exit onto Castle Creek Road toward the hospital and Ashcroft. Go 10 miles up this road to a large curve in the road, where there will be a large parking area on the right for the trailhead. (Ashcroft is another mile up Castle Creek Road.)

Trail Route: The trail heads to the right for a few hundred feet and then turns uphill, climbing steadily through the aspen forest via a series of long switchbacks. After about 1½ miles, the trail levels off a bit at about 10,600 feet, and very soon a large sloping meadow opens up above the trail, with a large grove of aspen almost dividing it in two. Deer can usually be seen somewhere in this meadow.

After the meadow, the trail enters a beautiful fir, and then spruce, forest, gently ascending, then slightly descending, into more aspen, back through spruce, and then up more steeply through another sloped clearing. Soon the trail skirts below one rock slide, and then across another large slide just before the lake. The lake is peacefully situated in a large bowl surrounded by rocky peaks, with large rock slides forming part of the perimeter.

19. Cathedral Lake/Electric Pass

Start/Finish: Cathedral Lake Trailhead (9,915 feet; 13S0343521E, 4323087N)
Destination: Cathedral Lake (11,880 feet; 13S0340578E, 4321581N) Electric Pass (13,500 feet; 13S0339496E, 4323566N)
Round Trip: (Cathedral Lake) 6 miles / 4 hours
(Electric Pass) 11 miles / 8 hours
Difficulty: Moderate/difficult (Electric Pass continuation is the most difficult part)
Elevation Range: (Cathedral Lake) 9,915–11,900 feet
(Electric Pass) 9,915–13,500 feet
Maps: USGS Hayden Peak; TI #127
Wilderness Designation: Maroon Bells–Snowmass Wilderness

General Comments: This trail is one of the most spectacular of all the day trips, climbing 2,000 feet from the upper end of the Castle Creek Valley through forest and along the canyon formed by the cascading Pine Creek, ending at a scenic lake at timber line, backed by the rocky walls of peaks close to 14,000 feet in elevation. The elevation of Cathedral

Lake is 11,880 feet, and rocky Cathedral Peak, which rises to the right behind the lake, is 13,943 feet high. A variety of vegetation will be encountered along this route, and wildflowers are abundant, especially along the upper portion of the trail. The trail is fairly steep, and the hike should be undertaken early in the day to avoid the afternoon thunderstorms which frequently appear quite suddenly in this area.

An extended hike can be taken to Electric Pass on the ridge beyond Cathedral Lake by only the very strongest hikers. Be aware that thunder and lightning is a common occurrence up here in the afternoons, so get an early start. At 13,500 feet, Electric Pass is the highest named pass in Colorado, and offers a breathtaking views of the mountains in this part of the state, including six of the nearby 14,000-foot peaks of the Elk Range—Snowmass Mountain, Castle, North Maroon, Maroon, Pyramid, and Capitol peaks. The pass was named in the 1920s by Forest Service Ranger Len Shoemaker, who was knocked down several times by static electricity while at the pass.

Directions to Trailhead: Take Highway 82 west from Aspen one-half mile to the roundabout and exit onto Castle Creek Road toward the hospital and Ashcroft. Go 12 miles up this road (about 1 mile beyond Ashcroft) to an unpaved road on the right at the green 12-mile marker. Drive .6 miles up this bumpy road to the parking area and trailhead.

Trail Route: The trail starts with a steady ascent through beautiful large aspen trees. After almost three-quarters of a mile, as the aspen thin out and intermix with some pine and fir, the trail enters the Maroon Bells–Snowmass Wilderness and meets the rushing Pine Creek, whose source is Cathedral Lake. In another one-half mile, cascading falls can be seen ahead where the canyon narrows and the creek cuts through the gap. The trail ascends more steeply, overlooking the falls, and eventually levels off in a rock field at 11,200 feet at the top of the gap. At this point, barren peaks over 13,000 feet in elevation can be seen ahead.

After a somewhat flat section, continue on a steady ascent through spruce and a large rockslide, until you come to a very steep slope with a series of short switchbacks cut into it. At the top of this slope the trail levels and you immediately come to a fork in the trail, with the right fork (marked by a sign) going to Electric Pass. From this point the lake is about 15 minutes away. Take the left fork, as the trail continues level. In about 5 minutes, stay right on the fork going up over a little ridge. At the fork with the sign to Electric Pass pointing right, stay left and cross Pine

Creek on a log bridge. Continue up to a shelf through the willows, beyond which Cathedral Lake is situated. Here several trails branch out and lead down to the lake.

(Electric Pass) For those wishing to continue to Electric Pass, double back from Cathedral Lake to the double log bridge over the creek and go left. You will come to a sign pointing to Electric Pass. A short uphill climb will take you to a well-worn trail, where you will head left to continue up toward the pass. As you head up, Cathedral Lake will be visible below you. Continue to the right (you are now above tree line in a large basin) and the brush gradually gives way to alpine meadows full of wildflowers in middle to late summer. As you look ahead at the rocky encirclement, Electric Pass is located toward the right, just to the left of a peak covered by loose rock.

While still in the meadows, the trail turns right and then takes a series of long switchbacks up the ridge on your right hand side. Cathedral Lake is constantly visible down below to the left, as are Castle, Conundrum, Cathedral, and other peaks in the distance. At the top of the ridge you will come to a saddle which gives you fantastic views of the mountains over the backside. Hayden Peak is just up to the left, and American Lake (not visible) is down to the right, hidden by some lower peaks and ridges. Many people think this saddle is Electric Pass, but it will take about another 20–30 minutes of crossing somewhat dangerous loose rock, and possibly snow, on a steep slope to reach the pass.

From the saddle the trail turns up the ridge to the left and works its way through the rocks toward the pass. Once you reach the pass, the panorama will convince you that the trip was worthwhile. Conundrum Valley lies on the other side, and the Maroon Bells, Pyramid Peak, Snowmass Mountain, Mount Daly, and Capitol Peak are all visible in the distance.

On the way back down, as you approach Cathedral Lake, a route (sometimes marked by a cairn) will go down through a gully to the left to take you to the main Cathedral Lake Trail, which you will intersect just above the steep switchbacks cut into the hillside.

20. Crater Lake

Start/Finish: Maroon Lake (9,600 ft; 13S0332175E, 4329503N)
Destination: Crater Lake (10,085 feet; 13S0329920E, 4328087N)
Round Trip: 4 miles / 3 hours
Difficulty: Moderate (extremely rocky trail)
Elevation Range: 9,600–10,150 feet
Maps: USGS Maroon Bells; TI #128
Wilderness Designation: Maroon Bells–Snowmass Wilderness

General Comments: The Crater Lake Trail is probably the most heavily used trail in the Maroon Bells–Snowmass Wilderness, and with good reason. Crater Lake sits right at the base of the Maroon Bells, two 14,000-foot peaks that may be the most photographed peaks in the country. The start of the hike is from Maroon Lake, the scenic foredrop to the Maroon Bells. Although the hike isn't very long, it is quite rocky, so good shoes should be worn and care should be taken during the hike. If you have extra time, there is also an interesting scenic route to explore at the south end of Maroon Lake. Make sure to bring a camera. Automobile traffic to Maroon Lake is restricted during the day (usually 8:30–5:00),

Hiking the Crater Lake Trail toward the Maroon Bells

and a fee is usually charged before and after those times, so the shuttle bus from Aspen or Aspen Highlands is the best way to reach the trailhead. Check with the Forest Service for the latest schedules and restrictions.

Directions to Trailhead: Take Highway 82 to the roundabout, about one-half mile west of Aspen, and turn onto Maroon Creek Road (which goes past Aspen Highlands Ski Area). Maroon Lake and the start of the hike are 9½ miles up Maroon Creek Road from the turnoff. During the summer the shuttle bus to Maroon Lake from downtown Aspen or Aspen Highlands should be used to get to the trailhead.

Trail Route: Go through the field on the main trail to the right of Maroon Lake to the far end of the lake, where you will see trailhead signs and a sign about the "Deadly Bells". Just past this sign, stay right on the Crater Lake Trail as it traverses up through the trees. At the next trail junction stay straight toward Crater Lake. This well-traveled, rocky trail ascends through aspen, spruce, and rock fields directly toward the Maroon Bells, which stand out prominently ahead. The trail will top out on a rocky rise and start descending as you see Crater Lake ahead. At the fork in the trail, about 200 feet into the woods, stay left on the West Maroon Trail to Crater Lake, which is just a couple of minutes ahead.

21. Buckskin Pass

Start/Finish: Maroon Lake (9,600 ft; 13S0332175E, 4329503N)
Destination: Buckskin Pass (12,500 feet; 13S0327709E, 4330005N)
Round Trip: 10 miles / 6–7 hours
Difficulty: Moderate/difficult (steepness and distance)
Elevation Range: 9,580–12,500 feet
Maps: USGS Maroon Bells; TI #128
Wilderness Designation: Maroon Bells–Snowmass Wilderness

General Comments: The trip to Buckskin Pass on this beautiful, very popular, well-worn route is a great long day hike that involves a gain in elevation of almost 3,000 feet. It is imperative to start early to avoid the usual thunderstorms on the pass in the early afternoon. The first part of the hike is highlighted by views of Maroon Lake, Crater Lake, the Maroon Bells, and Pyramid Peak. The upper part of the hike passes through a beautiful basin surrounded by peaks, and full of wildflowers. From the pass a panorama of Snowmass Lake, 14,092-foot Snowmass Mountain, 14,130-foot Capitol Peak, Mount Daly, and other prominent peaks unfolds to the west.

Directions to Trailhead: (Same as to Crater Lake, #20)

Trail Route: Go through the field on the main trail to the right of Maroon Lake to the far end of the lake, where you will see trailhead signs and a sign about the "Deadly Bells". Just past this sign, you will come to a sign indicating the Scenic Route Trail to the left and Crater Lake to the right. Stay right on the Crater Lake Trail as it traverses up through the trees. At the next trail junction stay straight toward Crater Lake. This well-traveled, very rocky trail ascends through aspen, spruce,

Buckskin Pass and the scenic basin lying below the pass.

and rock fields directly toward the Maroon Bells, which stand out prominently ahead. The trail will reach the top of a rocky rise and start descending as you see Crater Lake ahead. At the fork in the trail, about 200 feet into the woods just before Crater Lake (West Maroon Trail goes left), go right up the hill on the Maroon–Snowmass Trail. Follow this trail up through the aspen as it parallels Crater Lake, and then bears right through spruce into Minnehaha Gulch, with North Maroon Peak looming above on the left. Stay on the main trail through this fairly steep ascent— many side trails cut off to camping sites. In less than a mile you will cross a creek, and in another 20–25 minutes you will emerge from the gulch into a large, beautiful basin with Buckskin Pass (marked by a snow cornice until late in the summer) on a rocky ridge ahead.

Your climb continues through rocks, scrub growth, meadows, and past a couple of cascading streams. About 15–20 minutes beyond the top of Minnehaha Gulch you will come to a well-signed fork in the trail. The left trail goes to Buckskin Pass, and the right trail goes to Willow Pass and Willow Lake. Stay left toward Buckskin Pass for a steady climb through alpine meadows full of wildflowers. (Note: Strong hikers with two hours of extra time and an early start have an option of taking the route to 12,600-foot Willow Pass and Willow Lake, located in a beautiful wildflower-filled, peak encircled basin. If you skip Buckskin Pass, the trip to Willow Lake from Maroon Lake is 13 miles round trip).

The last section of trail to the rocky Buckskin Pass switchbacks somewhat steeply through some rocks and slopes which are bespeckled by a variety of wildflowers. When you finally reach the pass, the vistas in every direction make the trip very worthwhile.

22. West Maroon Pass

Start/Finish: Maroon Lake (9,600 feet; 13S0332175E, 4329503N)
Destination: West Maroon Pass (12,505 feet; 13S0327135E, 4322660N)
Round Trip: 14 miles / 8 hours
Difficulty: Moderate/difficult (distance and elevation gain)
Elevation Range: 9,600–12,505 feet
Maps: USGS Maroon Bells; TI #128
Wilderness Designation: Maroon Bells–Snowmass Wilderness

General Comments: The trail to West Maroon Pass follows a classic valley route and offers great wildflower viewing, a close-up look at the Maroon Bells, and a chance to see the Elk Mountain Range from a spectacular 12,505-foot mountain pass. Only the very athletic and fit go all the way to the pass on a day hike (with a very early start). However, a hike part way up the trail is an excellent day trip. Early in the summer, when the water is high, the two stream crossings may be impassible or treacherous to cross, so be prepared.

Directions to Trailhead: Take Highway 82 about one-half mile west of Aspen to the roundabout and turn onto Maroon Creek Road (which goes past Aspen Highlands Ski Area). Maroon Lake and the start of the hike are 9½ miles up Maroon Creek Road from the turnoff. During the summer the road is closed to car traffic from 8:30 to 5:00, so the shuttle bus to Maroon Lake from downtown Aspen or Aspen Highlands should be used to get to the trailhead. Check with the Forest Service on the latest status of access and parking.

Trail Route: Go through the field on the main trail to the right of Maroon Lake to the far end of the lake, where you will see trailhead signs and a sign about the "Deadly Bells". Just past this sign, you will come to a sign indicating the Scenic Route Trail to the left and Crater Lake to the right. Stay right on the Crater Lake Trail as it traverses up through the trees. At the next trail junction stay straight toward Crater Lake. This well-traveled, very rocky trail ascends through aspen, spruce, and rock fields directly toward the Maroon Bells, which stand out prominently ahead. The trail will reach the top of a rocky rise and start descending as you see Crater Lake ahead. At the fork in the trail, about 200 feet into the woods, just before Crater Lake, take the West Maroon Trail #1970 left, and stay along the right side of Crater Lake on the main, well-worn trail which heads toward the West Maroon Valley. For a few hundred yards beyond the lake the trail will follow the creek closely, and then head up through the trees, before climbing into the open valley through a rock field usually covered with columbines and other wildflowers. Ahead the valley walls are rimmed by rocky peaks with an occasional waterfall tumbling down.

About 1½ miles past Crater Lake you will come to the first stream crossing, where there's a good chance of getting your feet wet trying to cross. Make sure to go straight across at this point to pick up the trail directly on the other side, as it goes up onto a little plateau. After a pretty 25-minute walk through patches of woods, scrub willows, and wildflowers, you will have to cross the creek again just as the trail breaks out into the open.

The valley now spreads out before you as you continue on a steady climb for about 15 minutes to the last group of trees. From here the trail heads up somewhat steeply into the tundra through numerous

Hikers resting on West Maroon Pass.

patches of wildflowers. After gaining some more altitude, you will soon be able to see the trail in the distance angling steeply up toward the pass on the rocky ridge to the right. It will take a couple of switchbacks and a long climbing traverse to the top, where you will reach West Maroon Pass, engulfed in a world of rock and ridges. Hopefully, you brought a camera to record this occasion.

Snowmass Village/Snowmass

Snowmass (known as Old Snowmass) and Snowmass Village are named after Snowmass Mountain, a 14,092-foot peak whose basin, just below the summit, is a perpetual snowfield. Snowmass Lake, at the base of the mountain, is one of the most scenic and most visited lakes (with the exception of Maroon Lake) in the Maroon Bells–Snowmass Wilderness. Snowmass Village, first developed in 1964, and open as a ski resort in 1967, presents opportunities for hikes right from the village, as well as being an access into the Maroon Bells–Snowmass Wilderness.

Hikes #23–25 are short and easy hikes that lead from Snowmass Village to the access into the Maroon Bells–Snowmass Wilderness, the East Snowmass Trail (#26), which can be taken as far into the Wilderness as time allows. The Rim Trail (#27) is also accessible from the Village by foot or local bus, and follows a ridge, giving good views of the entire Snowmass area and surrounding mountains. The Government Trail (#28) between Snowmass Village and Aspen offers unique recreational activities such as hiking, biking, running, snowshoeing, and skiing throughout the year, but is especially beautiful in the fall when the golden aspen leaves bespeckle most of the route. Hikes #29 and #30 take you into the Wilderness in and above the scenic Capitol Creek Valley, climaxed by 14,130-foot Capitol Peak rising above Capitol Lake at the end of the valley. The Snowmass Creek Trail (#31) follows another valley through the Wilderness, and leads to Snowmass Lake and Snowmass Mountain.

23. Sleigh Ride Trail

Start/Finish: Trailhead at top of Snowmelt Road in Snowmass Village (8,900 feet; 13S0330739E, 4341223N)
Destination: Ditch Trail trailhead at top of Divide Road (8,960 feet; 13S0329789E, 4341354N)
Round Trip: 1½ miles / 45 minutes
Difficulty: Very easy
Elevation Range: 8,900–8,960 feet
Maps: Snowmass Village Summer Trail Map; USGS Highland Peak; TI #128
Wilderness Designation: Non-Wilderness

General Comments: This level, wide, graveled trail leads from the top of the Snowmelt Road in Snowmass Village to the Ditch Trail by the Divide parking lot across from Krabloonik. The trail is mostly shaded.

Directions to Trailhead: From the Snowmass Village Mall, walk up Snowmelt Road to the end, where the pavement stops. About 100 feet beyond this point the signed Sleigh Ride Trail takes off to the right. There is no parking at the trailhead.

Trail Route: Follow the trail as it goes level through the trees, traversing the side of the mountain. In 15–20 minutes you come to the Nature Trail on the right. About 3 minutes past this you reach the Divide parking lot. The Ditch Trail leaves out of the end of the parking lot.

24. Nature Trail

Start/Finish: Parking Lot 8, Snowmass Village Mall (8,650 feet; 13S0331166E, 4341593N)
Destination: Ditch Trail trailhead at top of Divide Road (8,960 feet; 13S0329789E, 4341354N)
Round Trip: 2 miles / 1 hour
Difficulty: Easy/moderate (rocky footing in places)
Elevation Range: 8,650–8,960 feet
Maps: Snowmass Village Summer Trail Map; USGS Highland Peak; TI #128
Wilderness Designation: Non-Wilderness

General Comments: This trail provides an access to the Ditch Trail from the Snowmass Village Mall, and is also an interesting short trail in its own right. Nature Trail walks are conducted along this trail.

Directions to Trailhead: The trailhead is located at the end of Parking Lot 8 across from Elbert Lane in the Snowmass Village Mall.

Trail Route: The Nature Trail traverses gently through the conifer and aspen along a creek, and encounters wildflowers and various vegetation along the way. After 10 minutes you come to a couple of picnic tables, beyond which the trail heads more uphill along the creek, winding steadily uphill through the woods and wildflowers (lots of columbine). In 15–20 minutes beyond the picnic tables, you reach the intersection with the Sleigh Ride Trail. Stay right on the Sleigh Ride Trail for about 3 minutes to the parking lot and the trailhead for the Ditch Trail.

Start of the Ditch Trail at the end of the Divide parking lot.

25. Ditch Trail

Start/Finish: Parking lot at top of Divide Road (8,960 feet; 13S0329789E, 4341354N)
Destination: East Snowmass Trail junction (9,120 feet; 13S0328489E, 4339855N)
Round Trip: 3½ miles / 1½ – 2 hours
Difficulty: Easy
Elevation Range: 8,960–9,120 feet
Maps: Snowmass Village Summer Trail Map; USGS Highland Peak; TI #128
Wilderness Designation: Non-Wilderness

General Comments: The Ditch Trail serves as an access to the East Snowmass Trail from Snowmass Village, but it is also a great hike on its own for those looking for a pleasant, shorter hike from the Village. The Ditch Trail can be accessed from the trailhead at the parking area at the top of Divide Road across from Krabloonik, or from the Snowmass Village Mall via the Sleigh Ride Trail (#23) or the Nature Trail (#24).

Directions to Trailhead: Take Brush Creek Road to Divide Road (.4 miles from the Snowmass Village Mall, 5.4 miles from Highway 82). Go up Divide Road one mile and left into the parking lot (avoid private roads) where the trailhead is located.

Trail Route: Take the fairly level trail as it crosses the Campground ski runs and follows an old irrigation ditch through the aspen, with Snowmass Creek Valley off to the right. In 10–15 minutes you will pass the Connector Trail going up to the left. In another 10–15 minutes you reach a corner where a bench is situated for enjoying the view of the valley and Mount Daly. Snowmass Creek is far below, and East Snowmass Creek is up to the left.

Follow the road up to the left until you come to the signed intersection of the West Government Trail going left. Stay straight on the Ditch Trail (an old road) as it goes through tall conifers, then drops gently into the East Snowmass Creek Valley, and then gently climbs up the valley with the creek on the right. Shortly you will come to the creek, with the old road going up to the left. Follow the trail right down to the creek, where there is a trailhead register for the East Snowmass Trail and a bridge over East Snowmass Creek. To get to the East Snowmass Trail, cross the bridge and switchback up the stream bank to the junction with the East Snowmass Trail right above the stream bank.

26. East Snowmass Trail

Start/Finish: Ditch Trail parking lot at top of Divide Road (8,960 feet; 13S0329789E, 4341354N)
Destination: East Snowmass Creek Basin (11,500 feet)
Round Trip: 11–12 miles / 7–8 hours
Difficulty: Moderate/difficult (steep sections)
Elevation Range: 8,960–11,500 feet
Maps: USGS Highland Peak; TI #128
Wilderness Designation: Maroon Bells–Snowmass Wilderness

General Comments: The East Snowmass Creek Valley is located between the Snowmass Ski Area and the popular Snowmass Creek Valley, and is overlooked by most hikers. This all-day hike, which is easily accessed on foot from Snowmass Village via the Ditch Trail (#25) from Krabloonik, or via the Sleigh Ride Trail (#23) and Ditch Trail from the Village Mall, will take you into the Maroon Bells–Snowmass Wilderness, into a true wilderness backcountry basin with alpine meadows surrounded by rocky peaks. It is not necessary to hike the full 12 miles to experience this spectacular Wilderness setting; the hike is enjoyable no matter how far you go. However, the scenery gets better as you get further up the valley, and entices you to keep going.

The trail is a fairly long, and at times quite steep, and covers varying terrain along East Snowmass Creek. It passes through evergreen groves and alpine meadows with great views of rock formations, waterfalls, red rock cliffs, and high rugged mountains. A watchful eye can sometimes see elk and occasional bighorn sheep or mountain goats in the upper part of the valley. Snowfields usually linger in the upper part of the valley until the middle of summer.

Directions to Trailhead: (Sleigh Ride Trail) From the Snowmass Village Mall, walk up Snowmelt Road to the end where the pavement stops. Just beyond this the signed Sleigh Ride Trail takes off to the right. There is no parking at the trailhead.

(Ditch Trail) Take Brush Creek Road to Divide Road (.4 miles from Snowmass Village Mall, 5.4 miles from Highway 82). Go up Divide Road one mile, and go left into the parking lot just off the top of the Divide (avoid private roads) where the trailhead is located.

Trail Route: Follow the Sleigh Ride Trail (#23) from the Snowmass Mall to the Ditch Trail (or drive to the Ditch Trail) to East Snowmass Creek (see description under Ditch Trail #25), across the creek on the bridge, and to the junction with the East Snowmass Trail #1977. Take a left onto the East Snowmass Trail as it heads uphill above the creek.

After a mile of steady climbing, the way opens up a bit and you can see the peaks ahead. In another 45 minutes you'll reenter the spruce in the middle of the valley and climb some more. After exiting this beautiful stand of large spruce and fallen trees in another mile, the trail traverses around a knoll and exits into the open, with the peaks around the pass visible straight ahead in the distance.

You will continue through some more trees until the trail stays out in the open for good in a large basin. Here the trail can be faded at points. East Snowmass Pass looms ahead to the left side of the pointed, rocky Buckskin Peak (13,370 feet). Anywhere in this area is a good destination and turnaround point.

27. Rim Trail

Start/Finish: South: Divide Road (8,620 feet; 13S0331031E, 4341809N)
Middle: Sinclair Road (8,540 feet; 13S0332766E, 4344058N)
North: Horse Ranch Drive (8,060 feet; 13S0333737E, 4344593N)
One-Way Trip: South Section (Divide Road to Sinclair Road):
3.2 miles / 2 hours
North Section (Sinclair Road to Horse Ranch Drive):
4.0 miles / 2 hours
Entire Trail (Divide Road to Horse Ranch Drive): 7.2 miles / 4 hours
Difficulty: Moderate (some steepness, but trail is relatively smooth)
Elevation Range: South Section: 8,540–9,220 feet
North Section: 8,060–9,000 feet
Maps: Snowmass Village Summer Trail Map; USGS Highland Peak;
TI #128
Wilderness Designation: Non-Wilderness

General Comments: The Rim Trail is a classic mountain bike route, but has become even more popular with hikers, because of the spectacular views from the ridge between Snowmass Village and Wildcat Ranch. The trail can be divided into two sections: the North Loop and the South Loop, with Sinclair Road (several parking spaces where the trail crosses the road) as an entrance/exit for the two loops between the north and south trailheads. Note that the North Loop is closed from 10/30 to 6/20 due to elk calving. It's best not to hike the Rim Trail when the weather is bad and storms are possible, as the ridge is very exposed.

Directions to Trailheads: (South) Take Brush Creek Road to Divide Road (.4 miles from Snowmass Village Mall, 5.4 miles from Highway 82). Turn onto Divide Road, and the trailhead is at the first intersection with Deerfield Drive.

(Middle) Take Brush Creek Road to Sinclair Road. Go 1.2 miles up Sinclair Road to the trailheads for the North & South routes at the end of the road.

(North) Take Brush Creek Road (car or bus) to the Rodeo Parking Lot. From here it is about a 15-minute walk to the trailhead. Follow the path along Horse Ranch Drive to the intersection with Rodeo Road. From here follow the gravel road/trail for about 10 minutes to the trailhead in the back end of Horse Ranch.

Trail Route: (South Section from Divide Road) The trail begins by switchbacking somewhat steeply up the side of the ridge above Snowmass Village. The occasional overlooks give great views of Snowmass Village, the ski area, the mountains, Mount Daly, and Capitol Peak. The trail winds through mostly scrub oak and lots of flowers. In about ½ hour you start getting on top of the ridge and have even greater views. At about 40 minutes from the start, the trail continues right at an intersection at the top of the ridge, but the trail to the left is worth taking as a short side trip, since it leads to another overlook. In the ground at the overlook is a memorial, a 22-foot diameter circle of polished granite with its component stones forming a helix (9,220feet; 13S0330598E, 4342193N). Down below to the south you can see a private lake.

Double back and pick up the trail as it continues along the ridge, and then down through some trees. Continue on the ridge, and in about 20 minutes you will be seeing Wildcat Reservoir and Wildcat Ranch off to the left. After another 30 minutes, when you come to a sign where the trail splits, take the recommended route on the right which traverses the hill. (The left route goes up steeply past a couple of houses on the ridge and then drops down steeply to intersect with the traverse route.) You will soon come to Sinclair Road.

(North Section from Sinclair Road) The trail continues on the other side of Sinclair Road. A sign at the trailhead for the North Route warns that this section of trail is an elk calving area in May and June, which is the reason for the closure until June 21st. The trail goes through scrub oak, serviceberry, and sagebrush, climbing a high ridge, where you overlook Horse Ranch on the right and Wildcat on the left. Mount Sopris, Capitol Peak, and Mount Daly are visible in the distance. The

The Rim Trail, with Mount Daly and Capitol Peak in the background.

trail continues to switchback up to the high ridge above Horse Ranch, with Wildcat Reservoir off to the left. In about 40 minutes from Sinclair Road, you reach the top of the ridge (9,000 feet; 13S0332985E, 4345532N). From here the trail starts its long descent through trees and sagebrush, as it winds down gently through the aspen toward Horse Ranch Valley. It then opens up somewhat near some houses, and soon you reach the trailhead in the back end of Horse Ranch. Follow the gravel road/trail to the intersection of Horse Ranch Drive and Rodeo Road. Continue on the path alongside of Horse Ranch Drive to the Rodeo Parking Lot.

28. Government Trail

Start: Snowmass Village parking area at top of Wood Road (9,150 feet; 13S 0331751E, 4340532N)
Finish: Aspen Recreation Center parking lot (8,080 feet; 13S0340068E, 4339265N)
One-way Trip: 8 miles / 5–6 hours
Difficulty: Moderate
Elevation Range: 7,900–9,460 feet
Maps: USGS Highland Peak, Aspen; TI #127, 128
Wilderness Designation: Non-Wilderness

General Comments: This hike between Aspen and Snowmass Village is popular with hikers, bikers, and, in the winter, cross-country skiers and snowshoers. The Government Trail (also known as the Brush Creek Trail) offers hiking opportunities in the spring and fall, when most other mountain trails are covered with snow. The trail is beautifully wooded with aspen and pine; a number of mountain streams cross the trail, adding to its picturesque quality, but sometimes creating muddy spots. The trail crosses the Buttermilk ski slopes, which are full of wildflowers in the spring and summer. In September, when the aspen are turning color and the leaves are falling, the Government Trail becomes a carpet of gold. The Government Trail (between Elk Camp Road and West Buttermilk) is closed annually from May 15 to June 20 for elk calving.

Since the trailheads are so accessible to Aspen and Snowmass Village, most hikers do this as a one-way trip and get a ride back. The easier direction to hike is from Snowmass Village to Aspen, which involves a loss of elevation. However, since it can easily be hiked in either direction, both routes are described below. This is one of the classic mountain bike routes in the country, so it's best to start your hike early in the morning when less bikers are on the trail. Please do not stray from the trail, since much of it is on privately owned property, and trespassing could endanger the future of the trail's use.

Directions to Trailheads: (Snowmass Village) Turn south onto Brush Creek Road from Highway 82, six miles west of Aspen. Go 4.7 miles to Wood Road (across from the Snowmass Center and gas station) and turn left. Follow Wood Road uphill for 2.2 miles to Pine Lane (marked private) at the end of Wood Road. Go up Pine Lane about 150 yards to the gravel road on the left for the mountain access parking. Go about 300 yards up the gravel road to parking on the left just before a gate and ski lift.

(Aspen) Turn onto Maroon Creek Road at the roundabout on Highway 82, one-half mile west of Aspen. Go one mile to Iselin Park and the Aspen Recreation Center (ARC) on the right and park (note certain parking restrictions). The old trailhead is at the south end of the tennis courts. The trail can also be accessed behind the parking lot at the back end of the ball field on the north side of the tennis courts. Some people shorten the trip by going over the Tiehack Bridge behind ARC, but they then miss the hike in and out of the beautiful Maroon Creek Valley between ARC and Tiehack.

Trail Route: (From Snowmass Village) Exit the parking lot and head down the ski access road, which then gradually ascends across several ski slopes and under a couple of ski lifts. At the fork in the road stay straight toward Elk Camp. Just after passing below the Elk Camp Lift, you will come to aspen trees at the edge of the ski area. Watch for the well-signed Government Trail which takes off left into the trees and descends. It crosses under a ski lift, then crosses East Brush Creek and a couple of smaller streams, before continuing to delightfully meander up and down through the aspen and evergreen woods and occasional small meadows.

At about two miles from the start, the trail comes to a large clearing and trail intersection. The Anaerobic Nightmare Trail goes off to the left, and the Government Trail continues through the open meadow toward Aspen. It soon crosses a stream with two logs as a bridge, heads up for a while through a stand of evergreen, and levels off through a peaceful pine forest after passing through a gate. At about four miles, in a beautiful grove of aspen, you will be walking along the right side of a cattle fence.

The beautiful Government Trail, carpeted with leaves in the fall.

The trail starts descending through the aspen, and in another one-half mile goes straight, as a faded trail forks down to the left. The trail then follows a rocky traverse (known to the bikers as the Rock Garden) before breaking out onto the West Buttermilk ski slopes. Do not head down the slopes, but stay on the trail as it crosses the slopes and descends through the woods.

After a few switchbacks through the trees, the trail traverses a Main Buttermilk ski slope (Chuck's Glade), follows some steep switchbacks down the side of a hill, crosses more Buttermilk slopes and under the Main Buttermilk lift (Summit Express), heads back into the aspens, and descends a few steep switchbacks just before the Tiehack Ski Area. You cross a dirt road (the ski road from Tiehack to Buttermilk), catching good views of Aspen ahead, just before coming out onto the Tiehack slopes. The trail follows the ski road a short distance before cutting off to the right above the bottom of the Upper Tiehack ski lift. As you leave the Tiehack Ski Area beyond Lift #5, you can see Iselin Park ahead with the ball diamond, the Aspen Recreation Center, the school area, and all of Aspen spread out in the distance.

From here the trail drops down through the trees, and traverses down to the right into the upper part of the Maroon Creek Valley. You come to the paved Tiehack Road, where the trail continues along the left side, then crosses to the right, until you come to a bridge high over the Maroon Creek Valley that leads to the Aspen Recreation Center and Maroon Creek Road. You can either go across the bridge and finish your hike (thereby bypassing the route down to Maroon Creek), or better yet, continue on the trail which drops below the bridge into the picturesque Maroon Creek Valley. Take a right on the gravel road that heads down toward Maroon Creek, and follow it for 7–8 minutes to a small footbridge crossing the creek. On the other side of the bridge, you will be taking a steep switchback climb up to Iselin Park and Maroon Creek Road.

(From Aspen) Follow the path around the south side of the tennis courts at Iselin Park, and walk down the steep side of the gully to the bridge over the creek. (You can go over the Tiehack Bridge from Aspen Recreation Center and skip the Maroon Creek Valley to make the hike quicker.) Just beyond the bridge go right up the gravel road for about 7–8 minutes to a road heading up to the left under the large bridge. Continue on the trail along Tiehack Road, and follow it uphill to the slopes of the Tiehack Ski Area, where it climbs through aspen, crosses the Main Buttermilk ski slopes, and climbs some more to the West Buttermilk ski slopes.

At the 3-mile point, the trail leaves the West Buttermilk ski slopes and goes through a rocky section (the Rock Garden) in the aspen. Continue up and head straight along the left side of a fenced-off area, as you stay above Whites Lake. You will be going through lovely stands of aspen and pine, and may encounter deer in here. At about five miles the trail starts dropping, then crosses a stream over two logs, and soon heads through a clearing. At the far end of the clearing a sign indicates that the Government Trail goes up to the left as the Anaerobic Nightmare Trail branches off to the right. Continue ahead on the Government Trail as you soon get some good views of the Snowmass Club golf course and the Brush Creek Valley. After traversing the side of a gully you will start a series of stream crossings.

After the East Brush Creek crossing, the trail climbs steeply through the aspen to the Snowmass Ski Area and the marked beginning of the Government Trail. From here follow the ski service road downhill, under a lift, and down No Name ski trail. Keep following the road down as it passes under two more lifts, then above the Wood Run lift to the parking lot which is accessed by Wood Road in Snowmass Village.

29. Capitol Creek Loop

Start: Capitol Creek Trailhead (9,490 feet; 13S0320494E, 4344819N)
Finish: Capitol Ditch Trailhead (200 feet past Capitol Creek Trailhead)
Destinations: Capitol Creek Loop (stream crossing: 10,040 feet; 13S0319738E, 4340373N)
Capitol Lake (11,585 feet; 13S0320327E, 4337003N)
Round Trip: (Capitol Creek Loop) 6 miles / 4 hours
(Capitol Lake) 13 miles / 8–9 hours
Difficulty: Moderate (more difficult for the trip to the lake)
Elevation Range: (Capitol Creek Loop) 9,000–10,240 feet
(Capitol Lake) 9,000–11,600 feet
Maps: USGS Capitol Peak; TI #128
Wilderness Designation: Maroon Bells–Snowmass Wilderness

General Comments: The two access routes to Capitol Lake make a good loop in the lovely Capitol Creek Valley. The Capitol Ditch Trail goes through magnificent stands of aspen and open meadows, and has great views of Capitol Peak, Mount Daly, and the Capitol Creek Valley. The Capitol Creek Trail basically follows Capitol Creek, and passes through splendid fir forests and fields of wildflowers, with great views of Capitol Peak and Mount Daly at many points along the way. The loop can be done in either direction, but going down the Capitol Creek Trail and coming back on the Capitol Ditch Trail, as described here, avoids a steep, usually hot, uphill climb at the end of the hike. Cattle are sometimes encountered in this valley; the beauty of the hike is worth this slight inconvenience. Very strong, acclimated, and physically fit hikers can also add on the trip to Capitol Lake, if they get an early start. Capitol Lake (11,585 feet) lies in a gorgeous setting just above timber line at the base of 14,130-foot Capitol Peak, and right next to 13,300-foot Mount Daly.

The Capitol Creek Trailhead, with Capitol Peak visible in the distance.

Directions to Trailhead: Take Highway 82 west from Aspen 14 miles to Old Snowmass and turn left at the gas station onto Snowmass Creek Road. After 1.8 miles, at the "T" in the road, go right on Capitol Creek Road. This road turns to dirt 5 miles from the "T", and at 7.2 miles becomes very rough. From this point 4-wheel drive high clearance vehicles are required for the last mile to the trailhead. If you don't have 4-wheel drive, park in the meadow on the right at 6.3 miles. At 8.2 miles from the "T" is the parking area with the marked trailhead on the left.

Trail Route: (Capitol Creek Loop) As you start down from the Capitol Creek Trailhead, you see the rocky Capitol Peak in the distance up the valley. Below is Capitol Creek. After a half-mile steep descent, you will cross an irrigation ditch on a log and soon get to the valley floor, where you cross Capitol Creek on a single log bridge, and begin a slow steady ascent through the aspen. Throughout most of the hike Capitol Peak will be visible ahead, as you continue along the left side of the creek.

As the trail opens up after a little over a mile past the creek, a tree-covered ridge can be seen ahead, over which the trail will go, and Capitol Peak and Mount Daly beyond. After cresting the ridge, you will come to a junction with the West Snowmass Trail, which cuts back to the left in some trees. Five minutes past this junction, you come to the signed intersection with the Capitol Ditch Trail, just about halfway to the lake.

Cross to the other side of the creek (usually a couple of logs are over the creek; you may have to wade earlier in the season), and go right in the meadow to pick up the trail angling up to the right. After a gradual ascent of about a half mile, you will reach a small group of aspen on a flat knoll, where you have spectacular views of Capitol, Daly, and the valley. From here the trail descends through some meadows and beautiful stands of aspen. In about 1 ½ miles the trail meets the old irrigation ditch and continues straight along the ditch through the aspen for a mile to the trailhead. (Note: Capitol Ditch Trail, also called Upper Capitol Creek Trail, Trail Reconstruction thanks to RFOV and Volunteers for Outdoor Colorado)

(Capitol Lake) For those wishing and able to continue to Capitol Lake from the Capitol Creek/Ditch Trail intersection: Continue to ascend through groves of trees and meadows filled with wildflowers. In another mile you will pass through a large open area, forested on one side, and with rocky walls on the other. The many fallen trees around you are from past severe avalanches in this area.

After zigzagging up a steep ridge, you will cross Capitol Creek at 5 ½ miles into the hike, and then cross back over the creek in less than 10 minutes. For the last mile you gradually get into rockier terrain as you pass through several meadows and stands of evergreens, and then go up through a small gully just over one-quarter mile before the lake. The trail enters massive piles of rock surrounding Capitol Lake as the lake appears ahead.

30. Hell Roaring Trail

Start/Finish: Hell Roaring Trailhead (10,005 feet; 13S0319110E, 4344515N)
Destination: Elk Mountains Ridge (12,075 feet; 13S0316198E, 4342473N)
Round Trip: 6 miles / 4–5 hours
Difficulty: Difficult (steepness)
Elevation Range: 10,005–12,075 feet
Maps: USGS Capitol Peak, Redstone; TI #128
Wilderness Designation: Maroon Bells–Snowmass Wilderness

General Comments: This fairly steep, scenic route up a forested ridge takes you onto a high open ridge above tree line at 12,000 feet, with spectacular vistas of the Elk Mountain Range, the Gore and Williams ranges, and the surrounding valleys. You also have the option of taking side trips to two wooded lakes, one with a very unique forest trail along a cascading stream. The Hell Roaring Trail offers some good photo opportunities of Mount Daly and 14,130-foot Capitol Peak off to the south. Although this hike is a little harder to get to than most, it is well known to the locals because of the spectacular scenery, both on the drive to the trailhead, and during the hike up the ridge. It is definitely a good workout, gaining over 2,000 feet in 3 miles. The trail continues on the other side of the high ridge down into the beautiful Hell Roaring Creek drainage and to Avalanche Creek, but this should only be attempted as an extended backpack trip by experienced hikers.

Directions to Trailhead: Take Highway 82 to the Old Snowmass turnoff (14 miles northwest of Aspen, 3.6 miles southeast of Basalt bypass light), and turn south by the gas station on Snowmass Creek Road. Go 1.8 miles to the "T" and turn right onto Capitol Creek Road. The road turns to dirt after 5 miles. At 6.3 miles there is a public parking lot, but a high clearance 4-wheel drive vehicle can continue to the trailhead. At 8.2 miles from the "T" is a large parking area and the two Capitol Creek Trailheads (9,490 feet; 13S0320494E, 4344819N), from where you have good views of Capitol Peak and the Capitol Creek Valley to the south. It is another 1.2 miles up the very steep road to the Hell Roaring Trailhead and parking lot. Unless you have good confidence in your 4-wheeling abilities, it's best to walk this last steep section from the Capitol Creek Trailhead parking to the Hell Roaring Trail parking lot.

Trail Route: At the Hell Roaring Trailhead parking lot, go straight ahead past a green gate and along the ridge past a pond. In 2–3 minutes you enter the Wilderness as marked by a sign. Following the wide trail through the conifers will take you to the intersection of the Hardscrabble Lake trail in about 10 minutes. The trails here form a triangle with four large fir trees in the middle, and the trail to the lake going off on the right. It's only a couple of hundred yards to the Hardscrabble Lake, a pleasant little side trip. On the main trail, continue up the ridge through the trees, enjoy the views off to the left, and in less than a mile you will reach a little knoll, where the trail begins to drop. As the trail levels a bit at the bottom of the short drop, the trail to Williams Lake takes off on the right. This side trip to the lake along a rushing, cascading stream through a pleasant conifer forest should be saved for the return trip, if you have time.

Enjoying the sights from the top of the Elk Mountains Ridge.

Continue climbing steeply through the conifers, with occasional views of Mount Daly off to the left, and other vistas off to the right. About two miles from the trailhead, as the ridge becomes rockier with fewer trees, you see Williams Lake below you off to the right, and Capitol Peak and Mount Daly to the left. Soon the high ridge ahead becomes visible, you go through the last conifers, and a huge, steep alpine meadow opens up before you, with your trail climbing up to the ridge. The patches of snow, usually present below the ridge until well into July, make for some good sliding on the way down, it you are so inclined. Enjoy the views from the ridge.

31. Snowmass Creek Trail (Maroon–Snowmass Trail)

Start/Finish: Maroon–Snowmass (Snowmass Creek) Trailhead (8,440 feet; 13S0327804E, 4340864N)
Destinations: Bear Creek overlook (9,520 feet; 13S0325781E, 4336386N)
Log jam (10,100 feet; 13S0326557E, 4333625N)
Snowmass Lake (10,980 feet; 13S0324500E, 4331740N)
Round Trip: (Bear Creek overlook) 8 miles / 4–5 hours
(Log jam) 12 miles / 6–7 hours
(Snowmass Lake) 17 miles / 8–10 hours
Difficulty: Moderate/difficult (distance, rocky trail, some steepness)
Elevation Range: (Bear Creek overlook) 8,440–9,520 feet
(Log jam) 8,440–10,100 feet
(Snowmass Lake) 8,440–10,980 feet
Maps: USGS Highland Peak, Capitol Peak, Snowmass Mountain; TI #128
Wilderness Designation: Maroon Bells–Snowmass Wilderness

General Comments: The Snowmass Creek Trail follows Snowmass Creek to Snowmass Lake in a picturesque river valley bordered by sloping peaks and rocky walls. The trail is mostly wooded, but has good views into the valley, and of the bordering peaks. The experienced hiker has the choice of turning around anywhere, but the overlook into the Bear Creek drainage, with the spectacular Bear Creek Falls against the backdrop of rocky peaks, is a sight that should not be missed. For those willing to cover 12 miles in one day, the log jam makes a good turnaround point and avoids the last serious climb to Snowmass Lake. Only the very fit, strong, acclimated hikers should attempt to make it all

The overlook from the Snowmass Creek Trail into the Bear Creek drainage.

the way to Snowmass Lake and back in one day. This trip is really best done as a backpack trip. Snowmass Lake (10,980 feet) lies in a beautiful setting with Snowmass Mountain, Hagerman Peak, and Snowmass Peak as a backdrop.

Directions to Trailhead: (From Aspen/Snowmass Village) Take Highway 82 west from Aspen 6 miles to the Snowmass Village turnoff on the left at the stoplight (Brush Creek Road). Take Brush Creek Road 5.4 miles to Divide Road and turn right (from the Snowmass Village Mall, take Brush Creek Road .4 miles to Divide Road and turn left). After passing Krabloonik (.9 miles), the now unpaved, somewhat rough road continues down, crossing part of the Snowmass Ski Area. At 1.6 miles from Krabloonik there is a fork to the right, but stay straight and go .4 miles to a parking lot at the end of the road. The trailhead is on the left in the trees.

(From Old Snowmass, 14 miles west of Aspen) From Highway 82 at Old Snowmass, go south on Snowmass Creek Road at the gas station to the "T" intersection at 1.8 miles. Go left on Snowmass Creek Road. At 9.2 miles from the "T", cross a bridge over the creek, in one-quarter mile turn right at another "T", and go .4 miles to the trailhead on the left in the parking lot at the end of the road.

Trail Route: The trail leaves from the left side of the parking lot, going uphill through the aspen. In 2–3 minutes you pass through a metal gate at the Wilderness boundary. The trail climbs a short ways through the aspen and conifers and soon levels off, as it follows the route of an old irrigation ditch. About 30–40 minutes from the trailhead you reach the first wooden gate. Snowmass Creek Valley and some old beaver ponds lie down to the right. In another 10 minutes you drop down to the junction with the trail that goes right to the West Snowmass Trail.

Stay left along Snowmass Creek, soon reaching a second wooden gate. From here the setting varies, with the trail going through woods, along the creek, and in the open with good views of the peaks ahead. The sound of the rushing, cascading creek is ever present. About 2 miles after the intersection near the West Snowmass Trail, the trail starts climbing steeply through aspen as it heads away from the creek, until it emerges in the open above the creek on rocky terrain. From this point (a great picnic spot) you have spectacular views down the Snowmass Creek Valley and up the side valley to the right at a dramatic waterfall created by Bear Creek. Rocky peaks, including the backside of Snowmass Mountain, rise in the background. Capitol Peak (14,130 feet) and Pierre Lakes are situated off to the right at the end of the Bear Creek drainage. This is a good turnaround point.

If you continue on, in another 1½ miles the trail levels off in a rocky area and approaches an old beaver pond, a marshy, grassy area which it skirts on the left side. After about 15–20 minutes you will reach a log jam at the beginning of a large inactive beaver pond area (walking across logs in the water—can be a little treacherous). This is the second good turnaround point.

Only the fittest and strongest hikers should continue to Snowmass Lake on a day hike. Cross the log jam and pick up the trail on the other side, where it heads uphill via several long switchbacks to get high above the ponds. After a steady climb through an old-growth conifer forest, about 1½ miles past the log jam, the trail reaches the junction of the Maroon–Snowmass Trail (which forks left to Buckskin Pass) and the trail to Snowmass Lake. Stay straight to ascend steeply along the right side of the rushing outlet creek for the last quarter mile to Snowmass Lake. A couple of waterfalls signal the end of the climb to the lake.

Basalt/Fryingpan

Basalt, located halfway between Aspen and Glenwood Springs, lies at the confluence of the Roaring Fork and Fryingpan rivers. Once a station on the Colorado Midland Railroad, which crossed the Continental Divide from Leadville and came down through the Fryingpan River Valley, Basalt now serves as the entrance to the beautiful, historic valley. The old railroad grade is now a road that heads over Hagerman Pass on the Continental Divide to Leadville. The Fryingpan Road provides a route for fisherman to ply the Gold Medal waters of the Fryingpan River, and for hikers to visit the lakes and other scenic spots in the Wilderness beyond Ruedi Reservoir.

The distances from Basalt to the trailheads of many of the hikes is 30–40 miles, a scenic drive which follows the Fryingpan River, circles around Ruedi Reservoir, and heads up branches of the upper valley. Because of the length of the drive, the Wilderness trails in the Fryingpan are infrequently visited by tourists, but well known to the locals.

The fairly steep Arbaney–Kittle Trail (#32), which starts at Holland Hills, is the most popular trail which is easily accessible from Basalt. Two hikes (#33 and #34) which take off from the lower part of the Ruedi Reservoir, about 15 miles up the Fryingpan from Basalt, introduce the hiker to the reservoir area, and the heights above it, on uncrowded, seldom used trails.

The remaining hikes (#35–38) all lead to spectacular high lakes in the Holy Cross Wilderness and Hunter–Fryingpan Wilderness. These lakes also offer unique opportunities for the adventurous to explore the rocky basins, cirques, ridges, and passes which lie beyond them.

The hike to Thomas Lakes (#40), described in the Carbondale section, is easily reached from Basalt, and is a very popular route for hikers from all parts of the Roaring Fork Valley. The lakes lie at the foot of Mount Sopris, and are aused as the gateway to climb this prominent peak.

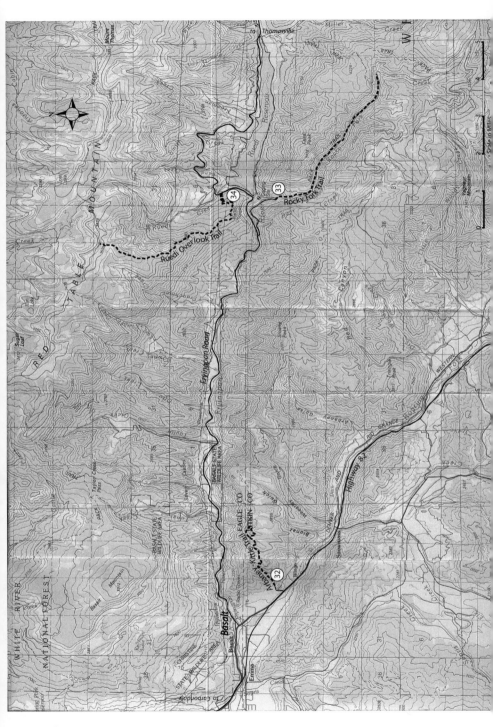

32. Arbaney–Kittle Trail

Start/Finish: Arbaney–Kittle Trailhead in Holland Hills (6,880 feet; 13S0326519E, 4358081N)
Destination: Overlook (8,320 feet; 13S0328277E, 4359194N)
Trail intersection for loop (8,510 feet; 13S0328693E, 4359105N)
Round Trip: (Overlook) 3 miles / 1½–2 hours
(Loop) 4 miles / 2–3 hours
Difficulty: Moderate (steepness)
Elevation Range: 6,880–8,520 feet
Maps: USGS Basalt, Woody Creek; TI: None
Wilderness Designation: Non-Wilderness

General Comments: This steep hike is very popular with hikers who are out for a good workout, and has the added benefit of rewarding views at the top. The spectacular sights include Mount Sopris, Capitol Peak and Mount Daly, and other mountains of the Elk Mountains Range, plus the Roaring Fork and Fryingpan River valleys, and Basalt. The normal turnaround point for most is at the first overlook into the Fryingpan River Valley, but a slightly longer loop is described here because of the additional opportunity to see more. The Arbaney–Kittle Trail can also be followed for miles towards Woody Creek. It's best to do this trail early in the day when it's shaded and cool, as the south-facing exposure can get very hot as the day progresses. Many people take their dogs up this trail.

Directions to Trailhead: Take Hwy. 82 toward Aspen from the main Basalt light (by the Texaco and roundabout) 1.4 miles to a left onto Bishop Road (by the stone wall) into Holland Hills. Take the first left onto Holland Hills Drive and go left up a short steep road (staying left of the dog kennels) to the trailhead parking, .4 miles from Hwy. 82.

Trail Route: The trail heads uphill quite steeply on a very well-worn, wide path through juniper, pine, and sagebrush. You will be following a gulch as the trail climbs steadily, with only a few less steep spots to catch a slight breather. When you reach the overlook (in about 1 hour), you are at 8,320 feet elevation and have good views into the Fryingpan River Valley, of Basalt Mountain, and of the Elk Mountains Ridge.

To continue on the loop, go up to the right, as the trail traverses less steeply with spectacular views across to Sopris, Capitol and Daly, Snowmass Mountain, and the other peaks of the Elk Range. In about 10 minutes you reach a high point, about 200 feet higher than the overlook,

A hiker approaching the first overlook on the Arbaney-Kittle Trail.

and the trail levels and drops gently. Early in the summer, wildflowers are everywhere in the scrub oak. In another 10 minutes you come to a trail intersection. From this point you can see the Roaring Fork Valley, El Jebel, Basalt, Mount Sopris, the Aspen ski slopes, etc. Going right will take you on the Arbaney–Kittle Trail towards Woody Creek. Stay left through the scrub oak to loop back to the first overlook. When you meet up with the trail, take a right to get back down to the overlook. From here it's a 40-minute downhill walk to the trailhead in Holland Hills.

33. Rocky Fork Trail

Start/Finish: Rocky Fork Trailhead below Ruedi Dam (7,660 feet; 13S0343266E, 4357900N)
Destinations: Valley beginning (8,250 feet; 13S0343440E, 4356608N)
Valley bend (9,450 feet; 13S0348604E, 4353340N)
Round Trip: (Valley beginning) 4miles / 2–3 hours
(Valley bend) 12 miles / 7 hours
Difficulty: Moderate (steepness for first part of trail)
Elevation Range: 7,660–9,450 feet
Maps: USGS Ruedi Reservoir; TI #126
Wilderness Designation: Non-Wilderness

General Comments: The Rocky Fork Trail goes up a rock-walled valley, beginning near the base of the Ruedi Reservoir Dam. The hike can be a short trip up a steep trail through beautiful trees above the rushing Rocky Fork Creek, to the beginning of a valley with abundant small ponds created by the local beavers. Many find this to be a good family fishing spot. Or, the hike can be an all-day trip up the valley to where it takes a huge bend to the right. The longer route involves a less than spectacular middle section, somewhat overgrown with vegetation, but ends up passing through a gorgeous forest, with Rocky Fork Creek creating a peaceful setting. The grass hillside at the end of the hike is probably the most unusual patch of vegetation that I have ever seen in the forests.

Directions to Trailhead: From Basalt, drive 13 miles up the Fryingpan Road toward Ruedi Reservoir to a gravel road on the right with a sign for the Rocky Fork Day Use Area. Turn right down the gravel road, and after .1 miles turn right across a small bridge. Go left on the road on the other side of the stream for just over one mile to the end of the road and the trailhead, where a restroom is located.

Trail Route: The trail starts up a narrow valley with rocky cliffs off to the sides, and lots of conifers. A short ascent on the right side of the creek for five minutes leads to a bridge, as the trail crosses to the left side of the creek and remains there the rest of the hike. From there the trail heads up quite steeply through a forest of tall conifers, with the stream down below on the right. After a little less than a mile of climbing through the beautiful coniferous forest, the trail starts to level off and continues close to the creek. As the valley opens up, you come to some beaver ponds, where you normally see trout in the water. You soon reach more beaver ponds and willows. This makes a good turnaround point for most hikers.

To make it an all-day hike, continue following the valley floor, as the trail is somewhat overgrown with vegetation for a stretch. Eventually the trail climbs up the side of the valley and traverses above the stream in a forest shaded by tall aspen and conifers. The creek breaks into occasional cascades to the right. After the trail climbs up above the stream and traverses in the woods, the valley opens up some more. Soon you come to a beautiful grassy hillside on the left as the valley and creek make a sharp right turn. Here the trail crosses the stream as a separate drainage forks in from the left. This makes a good turnaround point.

34. Ruedi Overlook Trail

Start/Finish: Ruedi Overlook Trailhead across from Ruedi Reservoir (7,960 feet; 13S0343504E, 4360108N)
Destinations: Overlook (9,180 feet; 13S0342537E, 4359669N)
Road 514 intersection (11,640 feet; 13S0341382E, 4365188N)
Round Trip: (Overlook) 4 miles / 2½ hours
(Road 514 intersection) 17 miles / 9 hours
Difficulty: Moderate (distance, some steepness)
Elevation Range: (Overlook) 7,960–9,180 feet
(Road 514 intersection) 7,960–11,640 feet
Maps: Red Creek, Ruedi Reservoir; TI: None
Wilderness Designation: Recommended Wilderness Area

General Comments: This seldom used trail, in a recommended Wilderness area, offers the best views of Ruedi Reservoir and the central Fryingpan River Valley of any trail in the valley. The trail passes through a variety of forest settings, the most spectacular of which are the tall straight pines. The route described here is out and back, so any distance from 4–17 miles roundtrip can be covered. Good viewpoints are abundant, and these serve as good destinations and turnaround points. The extremely strong hiker, who can get an early start on a good weather day, should continue on the route following the ridge between Ruedi and Frenchman creeks to the Red Table Mountain Road on top, where it culminates in some of the best views of the surrounding mountains in this part of Colorado. The trail is also known as the Ruedi Trail.

Directions to Trailhead: From the intersection of Fryingpan Road (Midland Ave.) and Two Rivers Road in Basalt, drive up the paved Fryingpan Road. At a little over 15 miles you will come to the Ruedi Creek Campgrounds and Boat Ramp on the right. Find a place to park (you may have to pay to park at the Campground), and walk up the Fryingpan Road another 100 yards to the signed trailhead in the woods on the left.

Trail Route: Head up the trail through the forest as it takes long traversing switchbacks to an old road at ½ mile. Go right and then back left onto the trail. Soon you will have good views of Ruedi Reservoir off to the left. One mile into the hike you enter a beautiful pine forest. Your ascent takes you past an overlook into the Fryingpan River Valley, and then at two miles, at the top of Red Hill, you come to a bend in the trail, with the overlook over Ruedi Reservoir. You can also see Ruedi Dam and the Fryingpan River Road down below. This is a good turnaround point for a shorter hike.

Further on, the views continue to be good, and soon the trail flattens out somewhat as you pass under some power lines. Beyond this, the trail starts a slow steady ascent, mostly via long switchbacks which follow the ridge in the forest, cutting from one side to the other, giving good views on both sides, as the trail occasionally comes into the open. At about 4 ½ miles into the hike, you reach a good viewpoint over Ruedi Reservoir, the surrounding area, and peaks in the distance. This is another possible turnaround point. The trail continues up the ridge via long switchbacks, moving from one side of the ridge to the other, mostly in the trees. At about 6 miles you come to the best overlook over the reservoir and to the east. The trail then starts leveling off as you follow the top of the ridge in the trees. At just over 7 ½ miles you start switchbacking up through fields of red rock on the final ascent to the road. In another half mile you reach the intersection with Red Table Mountain Road (Road 514). From here you have fabulous views in every direction of high mountain peaks.

35. Josephine Lake

Start/Finish: Henderson Park Trailhead on Road 501 (9,250 feet; 13S0363177E, 4356811N)
Destination: Josephine Lake (11,380 feet; 13S0365607E, 4360301N)
Round Trip: 9 miles / 6–8 hours
Difficulty: Moderate/difficult (steepness, length of hike)
Elevation Range: 9,250–11,560 feet
Maps: USGS Nast, Mount Jackson; TI #126
Wilderness Designation: Holy Cross Wilderness

General Comments: Josephine Lake, tucked in against the rugged peaks of the Sawatch Range, is a great destination for a long day hike. However, the camping, exploring, fishing, and sights are so good at Josephine Lake, you might consider backpacking in for the next trip. Expect to observe wildlife such as elk, coyote, deer, grouse, porcupines, etc., on your way to the lake. You will pass two parks (large flat open areas), Henderson and Coffeepot, where some of the wildlife can occasionally be observed. You're also not likely to forget the panorama of peaks and valleys that are visible from ridge on the last part of the hike. From the ridge, the Elk Mountain Range—Sopris, Capitol, Daly,

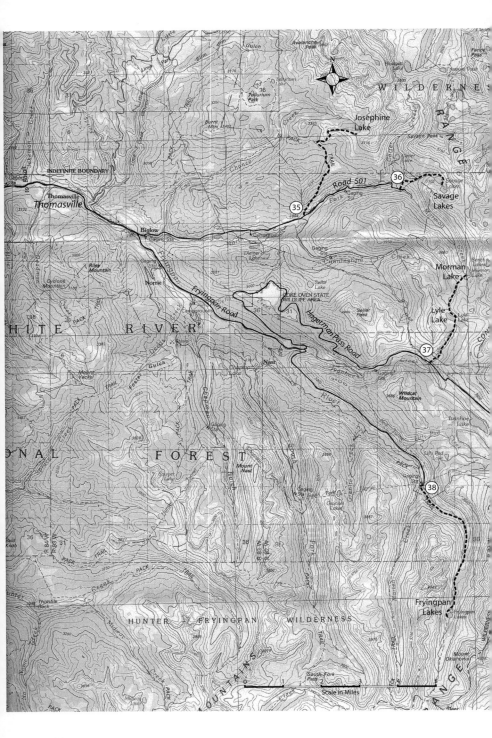

Snowmass Mountain, the Collegiate Peaks—opens up before you. Side trips from the lake, if you have time, include a hike up the ridge to Savage Mountain (12,191 feet), and hikes into the basin above the lake.

Directions to Trailhead: From the intersection of Fryingpan Road (Midland Ave.) and old Highway 82 in Basalt drive about 27 miles up the Fryingpan Road to a gravel road (Road 501) on the left (sign to Elk Wallow Campground), just before the road crosses the Fryingpan River. Follow the gravel road 4.5 miles (you will pass Elk Wallow Campground at 3.0 miles) to a fork in the road. Stay left on Road 501 (Cunningham Creek Road goes right), and in one-tenth of a mile on the left will be a small wooden sign (very easy to miss) for the Henderson Park Trailhead, Trail #1917. It takes about an hour to reach the trailhead from Basalt.

Josephine Lake as seen before dropping down the steep trail to the lake.

Trail Route: The first part of the hike is a climb through aspen, grassy areas with wildflowers, and then beautiful woods of tall aspen with ferns on the forest floor. After about 1½ miles you will come to a large, sloped clearing full of wildflowers and other vegetation. A little beyond this clearing in the conifers, when you come to the trail junction with the Carter Basin Trail (probably no sign) on your right, stay straight on the left side of the creek.

In a little over 100 yards from the trail junction you will reach the very flat, open area of Henderson Park, a marshy meadow surrounded by conifers. Ahead you can see a long ridge leading to the barren Savage Mountain—the ridge you will be climbing the last part of the hike. Stay left on the trail in the woods, which follows the edge of the open area, and then rises up away from the park. In about 15 minutes from Henderson Park the trail comes up over a little rise and drops down to another clearing, Coffeepot Park. Stay on the trail in the woods alongside the park. At the far end of the park, just about 100 feet beyond the park, you will come to a trail intersection (easily missed) with wooden signs on a tree. The trail to Last Chance goes straight, while the trail to Josephine Lake goes to the right. Take the right as the trail gradually ascends, traversing the side of a ridge, and then climbs more steeply up the ridge through spruce and pine toward Savage Mountain.

After a beautiful walk up the ridge for about 1½ miles, you will come to a trail going down the steep, north face of the ridge to Josephine Lake, which is visible below you. Use caution descending the steep gravely trail and you will reach the lake in 5–10 minutes. If you have the time to hike up the ridge to Savage Mountain, you will have great views of Carter Basin on the other side, and the many peaks and lakes in the distance, including Savage Lakes and Mormon Lake.

36. Savage Lakes

Start/Finish: Savage Lakes Trailhead on Road 501 (9,890 feet; 13S0367315E, 4357787N)
Destination: Savage Lakes (11,150 feet; 13S0369094E, 4357943N)
Round Trip: 4 miles / 3 hours
Difficulty: Moderate (steepness, but a relatively short hike)
Elevation Range: 9,890–11,150 feet
Maps: USGS Nast; TI #126
Wilderness Designation: Holy Cross Wilderness

General Comments: The relatively short Savage Lakes Trail takes you to a pair of lakes at timber line in one of the finest wilderness settings in the Fryingpan River Valley. These two lakes, one set at about 100 feet higher elevation than the other, are nestled up against a rocky basin and ridge, offering opportunities for further hiking, climbing, and exploration. The fairly steep hike to the lakes is scenic and pleasant, as it follows a gorgeous mountain stream winding through the forest.

Directions to Trailhead: From the intersection of Fryingpan Road (Midland Ave.) and Two Rivers Road in Basalt, drive 27 miles up the Fryingpan Road to a gravel road (Road 501) on the left, just before the road crosses the Fryingpan River. Follow the gravel road 7.9 miles (stay left at 4.5 miles at the intersection with Cunningham Creek Road) to the Savage Lakes Trailhead on the left and parking on the right. It takes a little over an hour to drive to the trailhead from Basalt.

Trail Route: The trail starts up the left side of the creek, climbing steadily through a beautiful conifer forest strewn with boulders. In a little less than a mile the trail levels off somewhat alongside the creek. Rocky cliffs and a boulder-strewn area lie off to the left; the trail is shaded by tall Douglas firs, and the cascading creek on the right creates numerous small waterfalls. The trail soon starts ascending more steeply.

About 200 yards before Lower Savage Lake, a trail to Carter Lake goes to the left. Stay right as the Savage Lakes Trail levels and passes through a marshy meadow. You will soon see the lake ahead as you drop down to the shoreline through the trees. Several big rocks jutting out into the lake make good picnic sites. On the other side of the lake is a rocky ridge, and the outlet stream from the upper lake flowing down through the rocks.

To continue on, go around the left side of Lower Savage Lake on a rocky trail. After about 5 minutes, at a split in the trail, stay left as the right trail just goes to the lake. In about 2–3 minutes, at the next fork, stay right (the left fork may be blocked off) and continue up over a short steep section to get to the overlook above the lower lake. From here it is only a couple of hundred feet along the outlet stream to the upper lake. If you have time, try exploring the basin up to the left of the lake—this involves a bit of climbing and scrambling, however.

37. Lyle & Mormon Lakes

Start/Finish: Lyle Lake Trailhead (10,745 feet; 13S0368338E, 4350287N)
Destination: Mormon Lake (11,460 feet; 13S0370008E, 4354085N)
Round Trip: 7 miles / 4–5 hours
Difficulty: Moderate (easier to Lyle, then harder to Mormon)
Elevation Range: 10,745–11,680 feet
Maps: USGS Nast; TI #126
Wilderness Designation: Holy Cross Wilderness

General Comments: On this trip you may spend as much time driving as hiking, but it's well worth the time. Not only is the hike beautiful and scenic, so is the drive, especially on Hagerman Pass Road. You will be overlooking the Fryingpan River Valley and Ivanhoe Creek from a road bordered by steep drop-offs. Try to imagine the trains taking this route over a hundred years ago! This road can be driven by a two-wheel drive vehicle, except for the last 200 feet to the trailhead, which can be walked. However, a high clearance vehicle is preferable.

The hike to the first lake, Lyle Lake, is an easy hike through a broad tundra valley. Many hikers stop at Lyle Lake, picnic or fish, and return to the trailhead. However, the most beautiful and spectacular scenery lies between Lyle Lake and Mormon Lake. This section is a real backcountry hike, with a variety of bouldered and treed terrain, ending at a beautiful lake nestled up against a steep, rocky ridge. You'll probably see elk and other wildlife while you're there, and the fishing is good.

Directions to Trailhead: From the intersection of Fryingpan Road (Midland Ave.) and Two Rivers Road in Basalt, set your trip odometer and drive up the paved Fryingpan Road. Stay on the main road past the reservoir and along the Fryingpan River; at 32.7 miles you will come to a gravel road on the right going to Fryingpan Lakes. Stay left on the Hagerman Pass Road (Road 105), which curves around to the left and turns to gravel just past this junction. At 36.2 miles stay straight on Road 105 as you pass a road going left to Diemer and Sellar lakes. At 44.0 miles you will come to the intersection with the Ivanhoe Lake Road. Go left up the short hill on the Hagerman Pass Road for 200 feet to the Lyle Lake Trailhead and parking. You may have to park below this short rocky hill if you do not have a high clearance 4-wheel drive vehicle. Hagerman Pass (11,925 feet) is 4.1 miles up the road, but a high-clearance 4-wheel or all-wheel drive vehicle is necessary to get there.

Trail Route: The trail begins with a gradual climb through scattered trees and lots of wildflowers, and continues through a tundra landscape in a broad valley marked by a rocky ridge at the end. After a little over a mile of very gradual ascent along the left side of the valley, the trail follows the curve of the valley up to the left as it steepens on its final climb to Lyle Lake. A large grassy meadow lies in front on the lake; rocky cliffs and a rock slide area dominate the right side of the lake.

To continue to Mormon Lake, cross the outlet creek just before the lake, and follow the trail along the right edge of Lyle Lake through a rock

Lyle Lake, a peaceful spot for fishing, picnicking, and enjoying the outdoors.

field. Stay close to the water. Occasional cairns will mark the way. As you get out of the big rocks and into the grass, watch for a trail fork, and follow the trail ascending up to the right away from Lyle Lake. It will take you about 15 minutes to reach the ridge above the lake, from where you can look back to the south and see Mount Massive and other peaks in the distance.

The trail continues on a contour along the slope of the mountain on the right, staying fairly level and passing through beautiful high country marked by rocks, wildflowers, scattered trees, and occasional streams coming down from the rocks above. Patches of snow often remain here until late in the summer. Although not heavily traveled, the trail is fairly distinct; however don't be misled by the side game trails.

After almost a mile you will see a barren, rocky divide ahead, and come to a pond in a flat area. Stay right of the pond and proceed toward Mormon Lake, nestled below the sheer rock faces ahead. Follow the ridge that leads down to the lake, and continue along the left side of the lake to the end of the lake for good scenic views of the Mormon Creek drainage beyond the lake. If you have extra time, the basin up to the right invites exploring.

38. Fryingpan Lakes

Start/Finish: Road 505 Fryingpan Lakes Trailhead (10,000 feet; 13S0367909E, 4344985N)
Destination: Fryingpan Lakes (11,020 feet; 13S0369118E, 4339722N / second lake)
Round Trip: 9 miles / 6–7 hours
Difficulty: Easy/moderate (more difficult past first lake)
Elevation Range: 10,000–11,020 feet
Maps: USGS Mount Champion; TI #127
Wilderness Designation: Hunter–Fryingpan Wilderness

General Comments: This route follows the Fryingpan River to three lakes—a lower lake and two adjacent higher lakes. The source of the Fryingpan River lies just beyond the lakes, below the ridge of the Continental Divide. This easy hike and the drive to the trailhead makes a good all-day trip. The 38-mile drive from Basalt up the Fryingpan River Valley alone is worth the trip, especially the last 6 miles on the gravel road traversing high up on the side of the valley.

The trail to the lakes goes through a V-shaped valley, bounded on one side by the Continental Divide, and on the other by almost a dozen summits over 13,000 feet. The treed valley walls are marked by avalanche chutes and waterfalls; the valley floor holds fields of wildflowers, boulders, and occasional debris from the winter avalanches. The trail to the lowest lake (10,900 feet) is easy to follow, and does not pass through any difficult terrain. Beyond that, the way gets marshy, rocky, and steeper. Great picnicking areas abound at all three lakes.

Directions to Trailhead: From the intersection of Fryingpan Road (Midland Ave.) and Two Rivers Road in Basalt, drive up the paved Fryingpan Road. At 32.7 miles is a road fork, with a gravel road to Fryingpan Lakes on the right crossing Ivanhoe Creek. Drive up this road 5.9 miles to the end of the road by the gauging station on the river, and park on the left. The Fryingpan River (on your left) and Marten Creek (on your right) flow together at the gauging station. A small bridge crosses the Fryingpan, and leads to the trailhead on the other side.

Trail Route: The route gradually ascends through a beautiful spruce and fir forest. After a mile, the trail starts crossing avalanche paths as it periodically emerges into open areas. Watch for all the evidence of the winter avalanches—the debris, uprooted trees, and open vertical paths with trees along the edges at various stages of growth. The peak you see at the end of the valley is Deer Mountain (13,761 feet), and the one to the left is Mount Oklahoma (13,845 feet), both on the Continental Divide. Many varieties of wildflowers grace the open meadows.

A little over two miles into the hike you will cross a small log bridge over the creek, and soon will enter some old growth forest. Half an hour later, after passing through some willows, you will find yourself at the bottom of a huge rock slide. From here, after going through areas of fallen trees, you reach the lowest lake in about 20–25 minutes. The meadow by the creek before this lake is an ideal picnic spot.

Beyond this point the trail gets more difficult to follow, as it passes through a rock field, and then, in the woods beyond the lake, through some muddy and marshy spots. The trail continues up along the left of the beautiful cascading stream through a pretty bouldered area. Large rocks offer good lounging spots by the creek. It will take about 20–25 minutes to hike to the second lake from the lowest lake. The second lake is surrounded by rocks, and the trail on the left of the lake goes through a field of large boulders with occasional cairns marking the way; the third lake lies just the other side of the second.

The two upper Fryingpan Lakes near the Continental Divide.

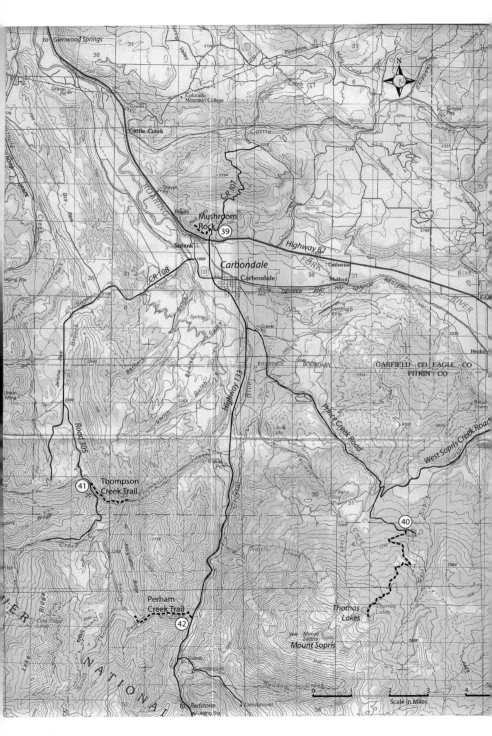

Carbondale/Redstone/Marble

Highway 133 from Carbondale leads up the Crystal River Valley to Redstone, the western gateway to the Maroon Bells–Snowmass Wilderness, and to Marble, which is bounded by the Maroon Bells–Snowmass Wilderness to the north, and the Raggeds Wilderness to the south. Redstone is a quaint town that houses Victorian cottages, the Redstone Inn, Redstone Castle, and many small shops. Marble is the site of the marble quarry, where the marble for the Tomb of the Unknown Soldier was quarried. Beyond Marble lies the old Crystal Mill, probably Colorado's

The Crystal Mill, near Crystal City.

most photographed structure, and the few historic buildings of Crystal City. This entire area has, in the opinion of many, some of the most spectacular scenery in all of Colorado.

Mushroom Rock (#39), located by the intersection of Hwy. 82 & Hwy. 133, is the local's favorite workout/short hike. Thomas Lakes (#40), at the base of Mount Sopris, is another perennial favorite, accessible easily from Carbondale and Basalt. Hikes #41 and #42 approach Assignation Ridge, west of Highway 133, from two different directions, and afford a glimpse into a newly Proposed Wilderness Area. Near Redstone, the two main western entrances into the Maroon Bells–Snowmass Wilderness, hikes #43 and #44, offer an easy and a difficult route into this gorgeous Wilderness setting. Beyond Marble, hikes #45 and #46 penetrate the Wilderness in an area marked by spectacular flowers, streams, and rocky high mountain settings. The Ragged Mountain Trail (#47) leaves from the top of McClure Pass toward a spectacular viewpoint at the base of Chair Mountain.

39. Mushroom Rock Trail

Start/Finish: Red Hill Recreation Area Trailhead (6,300 feet; 13S0308838E, 4365671N)
Destination: Mushroom Rock (7,030 feet; 13S0308137E, 4365963N)
Round Trip: (From parking) 2 miles / 1½–2 hours
(From trailhead) 1½ miles / 1–1½ hours
Difficulty: Moderate (steep and rocky, but short)
Elevation Range: 6,300–7,030 feet
Maps: USGS Carbondale; Red Hill Pocket Map; TI (none)
Wilderness Designation: Non-Wilderness

General Comments: The Red Hill Recreation Area is a trail system in a juniper and piñon forest, marked by the rounded rocks and red soil of the unusual geologic area known as Red Hill, located at the intersection of Hwy. 133 and Hwy. 82 in Carbondale. The Mushroom Rock Trail, undoubtedly the most spectacular hike in this system, can be linked with other trails in the system for a longer hike. However, this hike stands out on its own as a good workout for hikers and runners who like having Mushroom Rock as a goal, without dealing with mountain bike traffic, which is prevalent on many of the other trails. The trail leads to the outcropping

Mushroom Rock on top of Red Hill.

known as Mushroom Rock, where the views of the valley below are spectacular. Views of Mount Sopris, the Crystal River Valley, the Roaring Fork Valley, and Carbondale highlight the entire trip. Some of the other less steep trails can also be used to access the lookout at Mushroom Rock—see the map at the trailhead as you begin your hike.

Directions to Trailhead: Go to the intersection of Hwy. 82 and Hwy. 133 in Carbondale, and park in the park-and-ride lot on the north side of Hwy. 82. Walk up the gravel road about 10 minutes to the trailhead on the left. There is no parking on this road near the trailhead. A sign at the parking lot shows the trails of the Red Hill Recreation Area.

The view from Mushroom Rock of Carbondale, Mount Sopris, and the Roaring Fork and Crystal River valleys.

Trail Route: From the trailhead map at the trailhead, look for the Mushroom Rock route and start up the hill on the trail going to the left. You will be climbing uphill though pines and juniper on the red dirt, and through and around large red rocks. In about 5–10 minutes, just before a trail fork, you reach an overlook over the valley. The sign at the fork indicates Mushroom Rock Trail to the left and Blue Ribbon Trail to the right. Stay left and continue along the ridge. Be sure to avoid the trail leading along the left face of the huge rocks, as this trail is treacherous and deadends.

Continue following the ridge as you climb steeply over the large red rounded rocks, with great views of Carbondale and the two valleys off to the left. In about 35–40 minutes from the start of the hike, you will come to the high point and another intersection of the Mushroom Rock Trail and Blue Ribbon Trail. From this point follow the trail that leads out to the overlook, where some rounded rocks jut out over the valley floor. The trail drops a short distance to the rocks, and is quite steep with loose gravel on it, so use caution.

40. Thomas Lakes

Start/Finish: Thomas Lakes Trailhead (8,675 feet; 13S0316803E, 4352656N)
Destination: Thomas Lakes (10,260 feet; 13S0315239E, 4349292N)
Round Trip: 7 miles / 4–5 hours
Difficulty: Moderate (rough trail in places, mostly easy)
Elevation Range: 8,675–10,260 feet
Maps: USGS Mount Sopris, Basalt; TI (none)
Wilderness Designation: Maroon Bells–Snowmass Wilderness (at the lakes)

General Comments: The two large Thomas Lakes are located in the trees at the base of the steep face of the twin Mount Sopris peaks, a beautiful destination for a relatively short day hike. The views of the Roaring Fork Valley and the towering Mount Sopris are worth stopping for photo opportunities along the way. The last part of the trail is very rocky, and the Wilderness boundary is just before the lakes. The lakes have a number of designated campsites, and are a popular stopover for those hiking to the top of 12,953-foot Mount Sopris. It is best not to try to continue all the way to the Mount Sopris peaks on a day hike, because of the distance, the rocky route, and the usual exposure to thunderstorms and lightning in the afternoon.

Directions to Trailhead: (From Aspen/Basalt) Take Highway 82 toward Glenwood Springs to about 1½ miles past the Basalt bypass light, and turn left onto Sopris Creek Road. Go 1.2 miles to a "T" in the road and turn right onto West Sopris Creek Road. Go 5.6 miles to the top of the divide and turn left onto a dirt road, Road 311, toward Dinkle Lake. Exactly 2 miles up the road will be the parking area on the left, with the trailhead in the field on the right.

(From Carbondale/Glenwood Springs) Take Highway 133 for about 1½ miles south from Highway 82 in Carbondale to Prince Creek Road and turn left. Drive about 6 miles to where Road 311 forks off to the right at the top of the divide, and follow Road 311 for 2 miles toward Dinkle Lake to the trailhead.

Trail Route: From the trailhead you will join up with a well-worn old jeep trail, which leads to the right up through the woods. In just over a mile are some open meadows, with Mount Sopris standing out prominently ahead. Follow the signs to Thomas Lakes and Mount Sopris as the road contours left and then right past a side trail going toward Hay Park. Take time to look back at the views of the valley behind you. At 2 miles the trail enters the trees, and the rest of the way the trail goes through aspen, then scattered trees, meadows, wildflowers, rocks, with the constant views of Mount Sopris ahead.

About 10 minutes after you pass a small lake in the trees off on the right, you will come to a fork in the trail at the Wilderness boundary sign, and Wilderness registration. The first Thomas Lake is on the right, and has a very pretty aqua blue color. To get to the second lake and the trail up Mount Sopris, take the right fork on the main trail, which stays left of the first lake as it passes a number of campsites. In 5 minutes you will reach another trail fork, with the main trail going right. Stay left here, following the sign for Mount Sopris, and after a couple of hundred feet you will see the second large lake off to the left.

41. Thompson Creek Trail

Start/Finish: Thompson Creek Trailhead (7,250 feet; 13S0303629E, 4354751N)
Destination: Rock fins (7,050 feet)
Round Trip: 2–3 miles / 2 hours (or more for exploration and enjoyment)
Difficulty: Moderate (the first part is easy/moderate, then the trail becomes dangerous and difficult beyond the fins)
Elevation Range: 7,000–7,250 feet
Maps: USGS Stony Creek; TI (none)
Wilderness Designation: Proposed Wilderness Area

General Comments: This trail, which starts along North Thompson Creek, is not only a beautiful, scenic short hike, but it also contains some unique attractions. Of special interest are the rock fins—slices of rock formations about one foot wide reaching up into the sky. A small side canyon and a gorgeous rock-filled creek also add to the scenic beauty. The creek is especially an inviting setting for a lunch or break. The trail becomes less distinct and more difficult to follow beyond the fins, traveling through steep and rugged terrain, but those sure-footed climbers not afraid of heights can make their way to the remains of an old railroad trestle at the confluence of North Thompson Creek and Thompson Creek. Because of private property, the trail cannot be accessed from the east end; it has all but faded away there, anyway.

Directions to Trailhead: From the intersection of Main Street and Hwy. 133 in Carbondale, go west on Main Street (which turns into Thompson Creek Road, County Rd. 108). Continue straight, after the curve, past CRMS. At a little over 7 miles, take a left on a gravel road, Road 305, and continue 2.5 miles to the trailhead on the left, just before the road crosses North Thompson Creek. Use the parking area on the right across from the trailhead.

Trail Route: The trail follows the stream on the left, passing through tall conifers. At times the trail rises above the creek, hanging on to the collapsing stream embankment. The route is mostly shaded, as it passes through some scrub oak along the scenic, rushing creek. In 20–30 minutes you reach the first of the rocky fin formations above to the left. At one point the trail passes alongside the steep wall of one of the fin formations. In another 10 minutes you come to a side canyon on the left, a short side trip worth exploring. (It only takes a few minutes to get to a deadend, a rocky wall at the end of the canyon.) More large rock fins are evident beyond the side canyon, but the trail becomes more difficult to follow as it descends to the creek and then heads up steeply at a small gulch. This is the best place to turn around to avoid the high, dangerous route, which takes you above the river, and then down to the intersection with Thompson Creek and the remains of the old railroad trestle.

42. Perham Creek Trail

Start/Finish: Perham Creek Trailhead by Highway 133 (6,790 feet; 13S0307859E, 4349124N)
Destination: Large meadow below Assignation Ridge (7,925 feet; 13S0305315E, 4349050N)
Round Trip: 5 miles / 3 hours
Difficulty: Moderate (fairly steep with unsure footing in places)
Elevation Range: 6,790–7,925 feet
Maps: USGS Mount Sopris, Stony Ridge; TI #128
Wilderness Designation: Non-Wilderness

General Comments: Perham Creek Trail is a good early season trail, which is free of snow before most of the other trails in the area. This pleasant hike, not frequented by many hikers, gets the early morning sun, so an early start is feasible. The best turnaround point is a large meadow behind Assignation Ridge, with views of the South Thompson Creek drainage in one direction, and Mount Sopris in the other direction.

Directions to Trailhead: From the light in Carbondale at the intersection of Hwy. 133 and Main Street, set your odometer and drive south on Hwy. 133 just over 10 miles to the trailhead on the right, up a small gravel drive (somewhat hidden). The trailhead parking is about 50 feet off Hwy. 133.

Trail Route: The trail starts out of the parking lot by the trailhead sign on the north side of the lot. After switchbacking up through the scrub oak, it continues traversing up the hillside on the right above Perham Creek, highlighted by views of the Crystal River Valley. A steep ascent takes you into scrub oak and other vegetation, with Assignation Ridge standing out ahead. After about 45 minutes into the hike, the trail crosses Assignation Creek (with a small trail off to the right). The climb continues over the shoulder of Assignation Ridge. The well-worn trail is shaded by the aspen and scrub oak, with wildflowers usually in abundance. After about one

A fairly steep climb on the trail as it rises above Perham Creek.

hour from the beginning, the trail starts an easy climb up to the right away from Perham Creek and comes out into a large meadow (with sagebrush and other low vegetation) on the west side of Assignation Ridge. Deer and wild turkeys can often be seen up here. This meadow, with its views of Mount Sopris, makes a good turnaround point. Beyond the meadow, the trail drops down through a gulch to South Thompson Creek.

43. Avalanche Creek Trail

Start/Finish: Avalanche Creek Trailhead (7,360 feet; 13S0309972E, 4345137N)

Destinations: Hell Roaring Creek (8,160 feet; 13S0312117E, 4342308N)

Duley Park (8,480 feet; 13S0313889E, 4339346N)

Round Trip: (Hell Roaring Creek) 5 miles / 3 hours

(Duley Park) 11 miles / 7 hours

Difficulty: Easy/moderate (some steepness in the trail)

Elevation Range: (Hell Roaring Creek) 7,360–8,300 feet

(Duley Park) 7,360–8,480 feet

Maps: USGS Redstone; TI #128

Wilderness Designation: Maroon Bells–Snowmass Wilderness

General Comments: The Avalanche Creek Trail goes to Avalanche Lake (11 miles one way), and is a popular backpacking route into the Maroon Bells–Snowmass Wilderness. The trail follows the creek up a beautiful rocky-walled valley. I would suggest going at least as far as Hell Roaring Creek (5 miles round trip, just beyond the Hell Roaring Trail intersection) to see the creek plummeting down from above in a series of falls; if possible, try to make it to Duley Park. The well-worn, mostly wooded trail is easy to follow and climbs steadily up the valley, making this an extremely pleasant day hike.

Directions to Trailhead: From Highway 82 in Carbondale, turn south onto Highway 133. Drive 12.7 miles from Hwy. 82, or 11.6 miles from the light at Hwy. 133 & Main St., to Road 310 on the left with a sign for Avalanche Creek. Cross the bridge over the Crystal River and follow this dirt road 2.7 miles to Avalanche Campground and the parking lot at the far end of the campground. The trail leads out of the end of the parking lot; the trail register is 100 feet down the trail.

Trail Route: Follow the well-worn trail as it parallels Avalanche Creek on the left. In one-third mile you will pass the wilderness boundary sign and continue on a very gentle ascent. The trail is mostly well-shaded. About 10–15 minutes after crossing a side creek, as the trail starts ascending steeply up away from the creek, it enters beautiful stands of tall aspen and brings you through a wooded area, separated from the main valley by a knoll. When you come to the top of the ascent, you will see a small path leading off to the left; this is the Hell Roaring Trail #1960 (8,300 feet; 13S0312105E, 4342456N), which may or may not be

The Wilderness around Avalanche Creek.

signed. Keep going straight down the trail, and in about two minutes, after a switchbacking descent, you will reach a bridge over the gorgeous, cascading Hell Roaring Creek in a rocky gorge. This makes a good turnaround point.

To go further, follow the trail as it continues on a long descent to the cascading Avalanche Creek on the narrow valley floor. From here you will be passing through a variety of terrain close to the creek, with views of the rocky peaks ahead. A little over 2½ miles from the Hell Roaring Trail intersection, you will encounter a sloping open area, and in another one-quarter mile you will reach a large, grassy meadow. This meadow, surrounded by aspen and conifer, and highlighted by a stand of straight aspen at the far end, is Duley Park.

44. East Creek Trail

Start/Finish: East Creek Trailhead (7,725 feet; 13S0307161E, 4339069N)
Destination: Pass on the ridge above East Creek (12,130 feet; 13S0311906E, 4336496N)
Round Trip: 10 miles / 7–8 hours
Difficulty: Very Difficult (very steep)
Elevation Range: 7,725–12,130 feet
Maps: USGS Redstone; TI #128
Wilderness Designation: Maroon Bells–Snowmass Wilderness

General Comments: This seldom-used trail leads to one of the most scenic ridges in the Maroon Bells–Snowmass Wilderness, with unsurpassed views of the Wilderness and the Elk Mountain Range including Capitol Peak, Mount Daly, Snowmass Mountain, Pyramid Peak, and the Maroon Bells. However, the route is a very difficult, steep route, climbing 4,400 feet from the trailhead. For the experienced strong hikers, though, it's a very worthwhile trip through old growth forests, along a cascading stream with some waterfalls, and through a beautiful alpine basin to the ridge over 12,000 feet. A high clearance 4-wheel drive vehicle is necessary to drive the mile from the paved road to the trailhead, or this section can be hiked, making this an even longer, tougher day.

Directions to Trailhead: From Highway 82 in Carbondale turn south on Highway 133 and drive just over 16 miles to the North Entrance to Redstone. Turn left and go exactly one mile to the "Welcome to Redstone" entrance sign (on the north end of town), and turn left onto a gravel road, where you will see a sign "Access to East Creek Trail" after you have turned onto the road. It is one mile (high clearance 4-wheel drive) up to the trailhead, where there is parking for several cars.

Trail Route: The trail starts out climbing gently through the woods above the creek on the left. After about 10 minutes you cross on a bridge to the other side of the creek, after which the trail climbs uphill steeply on a rocky path. The creek valley is rimmed by rocky walls in places. In 20–25 minutes after the creek crossing, you come to a signed trail intersection at the Wilderness Boundary, showing Lily Lake Trail #1964 going right, and East Creek Trail continuing up to the left. The trail continues uphill steeply, relentlessly, into a beautiful stand of tall conifers, where the trail eases somewhat. A little over an hour into the hike, the trail crosses over a log to the left side of the creek, and soon starts climbing steeply again through the woods, soon switchbacking up along the left side of the creek. You come upon some waterfalls, and continue switchbacking back up to the left in the shaded forest.

Eventually, you enter a large sloped meadow (10,340 feet) as the route begins to open up a little. You soon come to a sizable waterfall flowing down the rocks ahead, just before the trail traverses left into the woods for more switchbacks. You cross East Creek again and soon come over a small rise, as a rocky ridge begins to appear ahead. The route starts leveling off a little as you follow the creek into a large basin below the ridge, which looms ahead. In the basin the trail disappears at times, and is non-existent in sections. Stay left of the creek and head up toward the ridge. As you get farther into the basin, veer left from the creek and head toward a low point on the ridge, just to the right of a rocky high point with rock ledges. You may come upon the trail switchbacking up toward your destination; don't be led astray by wildlife trails.

You reach the pass just to the right of the rocky high point, and have marvelous views over the other side of the ridge. The rocky peaks you see beyond the ridge include Mount Daly on the left, Capitol Peak straight ahead, Snowmass Mountain, Hagerman and Snowmass peaks to the right. In the distance, to the right of Snowmass Mountain, you can see the Maroon Bells and Pyramid Peak. If you have time, walk along the ridge a little—you will have good views down into the Gift Creek drainage, which drops into Avalanche Creek drainage. About a mile south on the ridge you can see Hawk Mountain, a peak that is visible from the Redstone area.

45. Buckskin Basin/Avalanche Pass

Start/Finish: North Lost Trail Trailhead (9,120 feet; 13S0314357E, 4327559N)
Destination: Avalanche Pass (12,110 feet; 13S0314631E, 4331335N)
Round Trip: 8 miles / 5–6 hours
Difficulty: Difficult (fairly steep trail and a number of stream crossings)
Elevation Range: 9,120–12,110 feet
Maps: USGS Marble; TI #128
Wilderness Designation: Maroon Bells–Snowmass Wilderness

General Comments: This hike climbs 3,000 feet, passing through Buckskin Basin, one of the most picturesque areas in the entire Crystal River Valley, to 12,110-foot Avalanche Pass. Over half of the route is above timber line in the tundra, providing spectacular views and meadows ablaze with wildflowers. The rocky knolls and rock walls provide both good scenery and a haven for alpine wildlife. Waterfalls cascade at points along the trail, especially in the early summer. Peak time for the wildflowers is normally the last half of July and the first half of August. From the pass you get a good close look into the heart of the Elk Mountain Range, with Capitol Peak and Mount Daly crowded by other surrounding peaks. Stream crossings could be difficult very early in the season during snowmelt. A 4-wheel drive high clearance vehicle will be necessary to get to the trailhead. Although the last section to the trailhead is a little rough, it is a beautiful drive worth taking.

Directions to Trailhead: From the intersection of Hwy. 82 and Hwy. 133 in Carbondale, drive 23 miles south on 133 to the turnoff to Marble on the left. Stay on the paved road along the Crystal River through Marble (another 6 miles), past Beaver Lake (no longer paved), to a fork 1.2 miles past Beaver Lake. The sign at the fork indicates Crystal City to the right and Lead King Basin to the left. Go left .8 miles (4-wheel drive high clearance needed) to the parking area on the right just before the stream. The trailhead for North Lost Trail is on the left side of the road.

Trail Route: The trail climbs initially to the left of North Fork Lost Creek through tall aspen with some conifer. After 15–20 minutes, at a trail fork, go right toward the stream (left is for horses), and cross the stream on some logs. The trail continues on the other side, heading up fairly steeply away from the stream through the tall aspen and conifers. About 25–30 minutes after the stream crossing, the way opens up and you can start seeing the broad expanse of Buckskin Basin. Soon the trail traverses back to the creek for another stream crossing in a narrow, rocky gully. From here the trail rises above the creek onto a narrow ridge full of wildflowers, with branches of the creek rushing below on both sides. A beautiful waterfall cascades down from the right.

About 15–20 minutes after the stream crossing you enter some trees, and soon come to a trail intersection, signed Arkansas Mountain to the right, and Avalanche Pass to the left. Stay left and follow the trail as it traverses into the open meadows of Buckskin Basin, and to another stream crossing in some bushes. One hundred feet past this stream watch for a somewhat hidden trail going uphill to the right. (There may be a cairn marking this intersection.) Go right up towards Avalanche Pass. Rocky buttresses frame the basin, with the creek flowing down through it. Wildflowers are abundant as the trail switchbacks up steeply through the basin, crossing the stream at various points.

Soon you reach the upper part of the basin, with rocky knolls, rocky walls, and the ridge in view ahead. The trail meanders up toward the pass, until one last steep climb takes you to a saddle, from where you can look into the Carbonate Creek Basin. To your left, 12,610-foot Mount Daly rises up . Follow a faint trail from the saddle up to the right heading towards Avalanche Pass. In about 10 minutes you reach Avalanche Pass, with the rocky peaks of the Elk Mountain Range ahead and to the right, including Mount Daly straight ahead, and Capitol Peak off to the right. (Note that you have one Mount Daly behind, and one ahead).

46. Geneva Lake

Start/Finish: Geneva Lake Trailhead in Lead King Basin (9,765 feet; 13S0319576E, 4327677N)
Destination: Geneva Lake (10,950 feet; 13S0320245, 4329502)
Round Trip: (From trailhead) 4 miles / 3 hours
(From Crystal) 8 miles / 5–6 hours
Difficulty: Moderate (some steepness, unsure footing)
Elevation Range: 9,765–10,970 feet
Maps: USGS Snowmass Mountain; TI #128
Wilderness Designation: Maroon Bells–Snowmass Wilderness

General Comments: Geneva Lake, at 10,950 feet, is located in a beautiful mountain setting, and is known for the fields of wildflowers which surround it in the summer, and the magnificent mountain waterfalls along the trail. This route also includes an optional side trip from Geneva Lake to another high alpine lake. Although the actual trail from the trailhead to Geneva Lake is not a very long one, the distance to the trailhead, and the difficulty in getting there on a 4-wheel drive road, makes this trip an all-day adventure that demands an early start. The trip should also include a stop in Redstone, which is located in the Crystal River Valley, and is the home of the Redstone Castle and Redstone Inn. Also on the way to the trailhead are the historic towns of Marble (so named for the quarry up Yule Creek which produced marble for many of the nation's marble buildings) and Crystal City (6.2 miles beyond Marble). It is highly recommended to hike the 2 miles from Crystal to the trailhead, rather than drive, since the road is almost impassable and can be very dangerous and difficult to negotiate. If you wish to drive to the trailhead (only in a high clearance 4-wheel drive vehicle), it is best to use the northern portion of the Lead King Basin route (see below) to access the trailhead, except when the road is wet.

Directions to Trailhead: From the intersection of Highway 82 and Highway 133 in Carbondale, drive south on Highway 133 about 23 miles to the turnoff to Marble on the left. Stay on the paved road along the Crystal River, through Marble (another 6 miles), past Beaver Lake (road now no longer paved), to a fork 1.2 miles past Beaver Lake. The sign at the fork indicates Crystal City to the right, and Lead King Basin to the left. Both roads lead to the trailhead and are for 4-wheel drive vehicles only.

The left fork, the northern route, is a little more precarious, but smoother if it's dry. Do not take this route when conditions are wet! High clearance 4-wheel drive is a must. At 6.3 miles from the fork, just after rounding a curve, there will be parking for a few cars on the left, and the trail will lead out of the parking area to the trailhead register about 100 feet further on in the aspen trees.

The right fork, the southern route (4 miles to Crystal City), is rougher (and almost impassable past Crystal), but includes the historic old Crystal Mill just before Crystal City (bring a camera). Therefore, most people use this route, park just beyond Crystal City, and hike from there to the trailhead and Geneva Lake.

(To get to the trailhead from Crystal on foot) Just under one mile past Crystal take the sharp left up the hill (a sign indicates Lead King Basin to the left, and Crested Butte via Schofield Pass straight ahead). In a little over a mile take the left over the bridge, and the trailhead parking lot will be about 10 minutes ahead on the right. The trailhead register is a couple hundred yards beyond the parking in the aspen trees by the curve in the road.

Trail Route: The trail starts out in a grove of trees, goes straight across a meadow, and through the aspen. When leaving these trees, you will be able to see the falls straight ahead. At the trail intersection 10–15 minutes from the trailhead, stay left toward Geneva Lake (Fravert Basin is to the right). As you continue up toward the falls, you will have good views of Devil's Rockpile

Pointing out 14,092-foot Snowmass Mountain from Geneva Lake.

(on the right), the North Fork River, and the surrounding mountains, including the back of the Maroon Bells. The trail will work its way up a fairly steep slope, and go left of the falls. Ten minutes before you reach the lake, the trail levels off and follows the left side of the outlet stream.

As you reach the lake, ahead on the right you will see a rocky ridge of peaks, just beyond which lie Hagerman Peak, Snowmass Peak, and Snowmass Lake. Just to the north is Snowmass Mountain. The trail continues along the west side of Geneva Lake and circles around the north end, eventually heading toward Trail Rider Pass and Snowmass Lake. If you have time, take the trail that traverses up to the left from Geneva Lake to Little Gem Lake (11,700 feet; 13S0320129, 4331237N) for a side trip of about 1½ hours.

47. Ragged Mountain Trail

Start/Finish: Ragged Mountain Trailhead (9,410 feet; 13S0301413E, 4331378N)
Destination: Viewpoint (8,960 feet; 13S0299548E, 4327485N)
Round Trip: 8 miles / 4–5 hours
Difficulty: Moderate (rooted and slightly rocky in places, route-finding skills needed)
Elevation Range: 8,800–9,685 feet
Maps: USGS Chair Mountain; TI#128
Wilderness Designation: Non-Wilderness

General Comments: This wooded hike, accessed from McClure Pass, culminates in a wonderful close-up view of Chair Mountain, and Buck Creek plunging from the spectacular Buck Creek Basin in a series of waterfalls. (Buck Creek Basin lies between the flanks of Ragged Peak and Chair Mountain). The route has abundant wildlife and is mostly wooded, so it provides relief from the sun on a hot day. Be aware of private property along some portions of the trail, and stay on the trail.

Directions to Trailhead: Take Highway 133 about 26 miles south from Carbondale (9 miles south from Redstone) to McClure Pass (8,755 feet elevation), and turn into a parking area on the left at the top of the Pass. Take the road out of the parking area on the left (Ragged Mountain Road—can be done by 2-wheel drive) for a somewhat bumpy 2.9 miles to a small parking area on the left in the aspen trees, just before a gate, and across from the trailhead for Ragged Mountain Trail #820.

Trail Route: The trail starts with some gradual ups and downs, and soon passes through beautiful tall aspens and into the evergreens. At one point Chair Mountain and Ragged Peak are visible directly ahead. The route continues along the Muddy Creek side of the ridge, crossing a series of small creeks coming down from the ridge and Chair Mountain. As you traverse the slope of Chair Mountain, you have occasional views off to the right of the Muddy Creek drainage. The trail is fairly well worn, and an occasional sign marks the route near small meadows. Orange diamonds on the trees also mark the route.

After about 1 ½ hours you come to a sign "Beyond this sign Private Land. Stay on trail marked with orange diamonds." You then hook up with a road, which you follow straight ahead (the route for #820 marked with orange diamonds on the trees). When you pass a shack on the left, stay to the right. You soon round a bend and have great views out over the Muddy Creek drainage. Continue on the road heading downhill, and you soon come to a series of ponds on the right and a cabin (8,920 feet; 13S0299755E, 4328211N). Signs ahead warn of staying on the trail and not going onto private property. You may have to skirt around water covering the trail at this point.

About 15 minutes past the ponds, the road breaks out into the open. A sign indicates the Raggeds Trail #820 dropping down through the scrub oak. Ahead you have a fantastic view of Chair Mountain and Buck Creek dropping over 1,000 feet from Buck Creek Basin in a series of waterfalls. Ragged Peak is partly hidden behind the basin. This makes a perfect spot to turn around. If you're tempted to continue down the trail to the creek, it's an uninteresting descent through scrub oak and vegetation, and really isn't worth the trek down and back up.

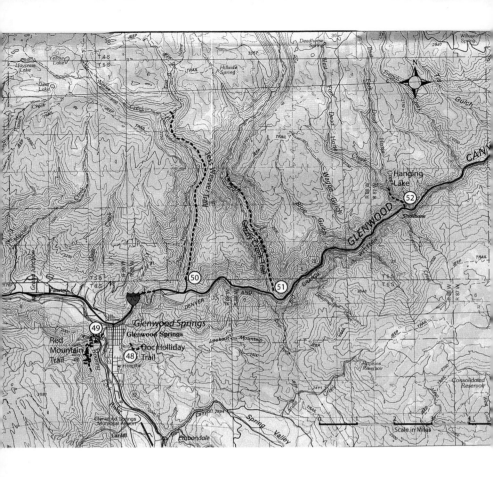

Glenwood Springs

When in Glenwood Springs, the town where Doc Holliday died, it is imperative to climb to his gravesite on a hill in the old cemetery overlooking the town. Everyone knows about the Glenwood Hot Springs and the Fairy Caves, but another site to be visited by foot is a huge cross, lit up at night, on top of Red Mountain. The road/trail leading to the cross also passes through the remains of the old in-town ski area. For those looking for Wilderness-like hikes, this historic town is also a gateway to the Flattops Wilderness. A number of streams, flowing from the Wilderness into Glenwood Canyon, have created scenic side canyons, which offer an introduction to the spectacular scenery of the Flattops Wilderness. Glenwood Canyon itself is one of the scenic wonders of this part of Colorado.

Hike #48 is the short hike to Doc Holliday's grave, and hike #49 climbs Red Mountain to the cross. The Jess Weaver Trail (#50) and the Grizzly Creek Trail (#51) both follow rock-rimmed canyons, whose creeks drain from the Flattops. The Hanging Lake Trail (#52) demands another superlative—the most spectacular short hike in the state, if not in the country. For that reason, it's also probably the most crowded trail described in this book.

48. Doc Holliday Trail

Start/Finish: Pioneer Cemetery Trailhead (5,940 feet; 13S0300497E, 4379423N)
Destination: Doc Holliday grave site (6,190 feet)
Round Trip: ½ mile / 30 minutes
Difficulty: Easy/moderate (some steepness, but short)
Elevation Range: 5,940–6,190 feet
Maps: USGS Glenwood Springs; TI #123
Wilderness Designation: Non-Wilderness

General Comments: The Doc Holliday Trail is officially signed as the Pioneer Cemetery Trail. The Pioneer Cemetery, on a hill overlooking Glenwood Springs, was first opened in 1887, and is where many of the early settlers are buried. It's worthwhile wandering around the cemetery to check out the nineteenth and twentieth century gravestones of many of the original founders of Glenwood Springs.

Doc's grave site in Pioneer Cemetery.

The sign at the trailhead explains: "Originally named Glenwood Cemetery, Glenwood's first burial ground was privately owned by mortician J. C. Schwartz. A wooden horse-drawn hearse brought early residents up this road to their final resting place. The hearse is now at the Frontier Historical Museum in Glenwood. Doc Holliday, in May, 1887, after gaining a reputation as a gambler and gunman, took up residence in a Glenwood hotel. He was in the last stages of consumption and died on November 8th of the same year. He was well liked in the town and his employers took up a collection and paid his funeral expenses. No one is sure of the exact details of his death. Some say that because a Midwestern gang wanted his body, a funeral with a casket full of stones took place and Doc Holliday was buried in the basement of a house at 8th & Palmer, and his body was moved to the cemetery several years later. No one knows officially where he is buried."

Directions to Trailhead: Take Grand Avenue in Glenwood Springs to 13th Street and go east for three blocks to a left onto Bennett Street. The trailhead is at the corner of 12th and Bennett on the right.

Trail Route Directions: The gravel trail climbs steadily up Cemetery Hill, with views out over Glenwood Springs. About 6–7 minutes up the trail, a sign gives information about Richard Sopris (for whom Mount Sopris was named)— the first white man to use the Glenwood Hot Springs in 1860, and about other famous visitors to Glenwood Springs, like Teddy Roosevelt and Al Capone. In a little over 10 minutes you arrive at the Pioneer Cemetery surrounded by a fence. Head to the left for Doc Holliday's grave, which is on the far west end of the cemetery. The inscription reads: "Doc Holliday, 1852–1887. He died in bed. This memorial is dedicated to Doc Holliday who is buried someplace in this cemetery." From the top of Cemetery Hill you get a good panorama of the town of Glenwood Springs.

49. Red Mountain Trail

Start/Finish: Jeanne Golay Trailhead (5,860 feet; 13S0299440E, 4379934N)
Destination: Large metal cross at top of old ski lift (7,445 feet; 13S0298692E, 4378621N)
Round Trip: 6½ miles / 2½–3 hours
Difficulty: Moderate (a smooth surface, but a steady strenuous climb)
Elevation Range: 5,860–7,445 feet
Maps: USGS Glenwood, TI #123
Wilderness Designation: Non-Wilderness

General Comments: The trail follows Red Mountain Road, which used to be the access for Glenwood Springs' original ski area, traces of which still remain. The road is a good uphill workout and leads to wonderful views of Glenwood Springs, Mount Sopris, the Roaring Fork Valley and Glenwood Canyon, and the Colorado and Roaring Fork rivers. This route has been named the Jeanne Golay Trail, dedicated to Jeanne Golay, an Olympic Cyclist from Glenwood who trained on this road and finished sixth in the 1992 Olympics in Barcelona. The trail ends at an overlook by a large metal cross, which is lit up during Christmas and Easter at night, and can be seen from much of the lower valley around Glenwood.

Directions to Trailhead: From Grand Avenue in Glenwood turn west on 8th Street, right on Colorado Ave., left on 7th Street, continue across the 8th Street bridge, right on Midland, left on Red Mountain Drive, right on 9th up the hill to the trailhead parking area on the left.

Trail Route: Head up the gravel trail blocked off to vehicles by several large boulders. Follow the trail as it cuts a couple of switchbacks of the road, and then get on the gravel road as it heads up Red Mountain to the right of the water treatment facility. In about 20–25 minutes you start getting good views of Glenwood Springs and the Colorado River below. After passing remnants of the old ski lift, you reach more lookout points over Glenwood and the surrounding valleys and canyons. Keep your eyes peeled for foot paths cutting some of the road switchbacks further up, or you can stay on the road as it switchbacks its way up to the cross. About an hour up, one lookout has a bench where you can take a rest. After passing a gate to private property, the road levels and you come to the cross and some antennas. This is your goal and turnaround point.

50. Jess Weaver Trail

Start/Finish: Jess Weaver Trailhead (6,040 feet; 13S0302989E, 4382181N)

Destinations: Bridge at 3¼ miles (7,630 feet; 13S0303995E, 4386436N)

Waterfall & bridge at 5 miles (8,500 feet; 13S0303059E, 4388130N)

Waterfall at 5½ miles (8,860 feet; 13S0302760E, 4388863N)

Milepost 6 (9,300 feet; 13S0302784E, 4389238N)

Round Trip: (Bridge) 6½ miles / 4 hours

(Waterfall & bridge) 10 miles / 6–7 hours

(Waterfall) 11 miles / 7–8 hours

(Milepost 6) 12 miles / 8–9 hours

Difficulty: Moderate

Elevation Range: (Bridge) 6,040–7,630 feet

(Waterfall & bridge) 6,040–8,500 feet

(Waterfall) 6,040–8,860 feet

(Milepost 6) 6,040–9,300 feet

Maps: USGS Glenwood Springs, Carbonate; TI #123

Wilderness Designation: Non-Wilderness

General Comments: The Jess Weaver Trail (formerly No Name Trail) leads along No Name Creek from Glenwood Canyon up into the Flattops, and is a route used by backpackers to access the scenic Flattops Wilderness. But this trail is much more popular with dayhikers, who can enjoy an out-and-back trip of anywhere from 1–12 miles roundtrip. The full 12-mile hike is described here, with the popular turnaround points being: the bridge a little past 3 miles, the bridge and memorial plaque (and waterfall) at 5 miles, and the spectacular waterfall at about 5½ miles. Distances from the trailhead are marked on wooden mileposts for every mile. The posts are sometimes clawed up badly by animals.

No Name Creek is most spectacular during late spring/early summer runoff, when the creek cascades over hundreds or rocky drop-offs. But the trail can be a pleasant experience anytime during the summer and fall. The trail is somewhat shaded, but it's best to start early during the summer to avoid much of the midday heat. Good, strong, experienced hikers can take an unmaintained trail over the ridge separating No Name and Grizzly creeks (involving a stream crossing at Grizzly Creek, which will be impassable during runoff), and hike back down Grizzly Creek to Glenwood Canyon, where they can finish the loop along the bike path.

Directions to Trailhead: Take I-70 east from Glenwood Springs 2 miles to Exit 119 (No Name Exit). Exit, and take the first left to cross the bridge over I-70. Take this road north (marked "No Outlet") .4 miles to trailhead parking on the left.

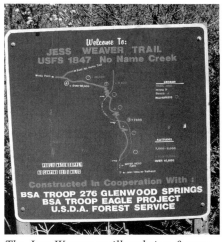

Trail Route: Walk up the road from the parking area about 100 feet to a green gate. If the gate is closed, you can bypass the gate on the right. From the gate, continue up the gravel road above and to the right of the creek. In 10

The Jess Weaver trailhead sign & map.

minutes you reach a Glenwood Springs water and power generation facility ("Public Water System, Glenwood Springs") with a small dam. Just before it, you can see the remains of an old aqueduct. After crossing over the dam on the road, stay right as the road narrows down to a trail.

The trail gradually ascends along the left side of the creek. About 5 minutes past milepost 1, go left uphill as the trail splits. A sign may be there, indicating "River Only" to the right and "Trail 1847" to the left. Continue through the scrub oak as the trail rises above the river. After regaining the river at 2 miles, the trail begins to climb more steeply and gets rockier. Cascades and small waterfalls are prevalent in the stream as the trail continues to rise. Just before milepost 3 is a good overlook on the cascading waterfalls.

As you continue, the rocky walls are more evident ahead, and just over 5 minutes beyond milepost 3, you reach a bridge. This is where the aqueduct from Grizzly Creek comes through to No Name Creek. Over the bridge the trail takes a traverse to the right, and just beyond the first switchback, a faded trail goes off to the right. (This is the trail that switchbacks steeply over the ridge and drops into Grizzly Creek —see notes under "General Comments"). Stay left on the main trail, which climbs high above the creek, giving good views back down the creek gorge. A rock buttress on the other side rises high above the creek. After passing through a grove of aspens a little before milepost 4, the underbrush starts to thicken. You see the canyon narrowing ahead, and at milepost 5 come to a bridge crossing the creek. Above are cascading falls rushing down, quite a sight. A plaque on a rock by the bridge states: "These bridges were built in memory of Jess Weaver who died here in a bad crossing on June 25, 1978. They were built with the cooperation of the Forest Service, National Guard, and a lot of his friends."

This bridge is a good turnaround point, but those with the energy and time should continue on the climb up the other side to the next waterfall. The trail switchbacks up and levels off somewhat. After about 20 minutes you cross a bridge just above the confluence of East No Name and No Name creeks. A short climb beyond the bridge gives you a great view of a huge waterfall on the left, as No Name Creek comes roaring down a several hundred-foot slope. A steep climb then takes you to milepost 6 at 9,300 feet, where you see that same waterfall from above, and the Elk Mountain Range and Maroon Bells in the distance.

51. Grizzly Creek Trail

Start/Finish: Grizzly Creek Trailhead (5,930 feet; 13S0306734E, 4381477N)
Destination: Grizzly Creek Crossing (7,745 feet; 13S0304938E, 4386577N)
Round Trip: 7 miles / 4–5 hours
Difficulty: Easy at first; Moderate/difficult as the trail gets rockier and steeper
Elevation Range: 5,930–7,745 feet
Maps: USGS Glenwood Springs, Shoshone; TI #123
Wilderness Designation: Non-Wilderness

General Comments: Grizzly Creek Trail takes you up a scenic canyon highlighted by spectacular rock formations and a cascading creek. The first part is wide and graveled, making it a good short walk for families. The trail eventually gets fairly wild, and ends at the creek in a narrow canyon flanked by rocky walls. However, at low water, experienced hikers may be able to cross the creek, and make a difficult connection on a faded steep trail to the Jess Weaver Trail for the return trip.

Directions to Trailhead: Take I-70 east from Glenwood Springs 4.5 miles to Exit 121, Grizzly Creek Rest Area. Exit, and continue through the Rest Area, following signs for I-70 east. Immediately after crossing Grizzly Creek take a left into the trailhead parking lot.

Trail Route: The trail, smooth and wide at first, goes along the right side of the creek. Spectacular rock walls and rock pinnacles rise on both sides. This section is another good spot for family walks. The trail narrows and continues on an easy ascent along the creek, as it leaves the river, and then drops back down to it about an hour into the hike. Ahead the river is filled with large boulders, creating many small waterfalls.

Beyond this, the trail starts a steady, fairly steep ascent to high above the river, from where you can see the creek far below. Rocky walls ahead close in on the creek, and at just under 2 hours, as the trail levels off somewhat, you reach a rocky face with the creek again alongside. A steady, steep climb, as the way gets rockier, brings you to the trail end at the creek at milepost 3½. A black aqueduct pipe can be seen on other side of the creek.

The trail seems to cross creek here, but is completely impassable at higher water levels. At low water levels strong, experienced hikers may be able to wade across

Grizzly Creek, as it rushes wildly over boulders through the creekside vegetation.

Grizzly Creek and pick up the trail on the other side as it climbs steeply up over a ridge and drops into No Name Creek. This weak trail is unmaintained and may be hard to follow in a couple of places. It's best to turn around here and retrace your steps to the trailhead.

52. Hanging Lake

Start/Finish: Hanging Lake Trailhead at Exit 125 on I-70 (6,165 feet; 13S0312439E, 4384797N)
Destination: Hanging Lake (7,180 feet; 13S0311878E, 4385780N)
Round Trip: 2.4 miles / 2–3 hours
Difficulty: Moderate/difficult (steepness and rocky path)
Elevation Range: 6,165–7,180 feet
Maps: USGS Shoshone; TI #123
Wilderness Designation: Non-Wilderness

General Comments: Hanging Lake, in Glenwood Canyon, was formed by a geologic fault, which caused the lake to drop away from the valley floor above. The lake edge is built from dissolved minerals deposited by the water. Bridal Veil Falls and Spouting Rock are two outstanding water features above the lake. The trail to this spectacular lake setting is so popular that it has its own exit on the Interstate, and a modern rest area with facilities and picnic benches. There is also a restroom and bike racks at the trailhead. When I-70 was constructed through Glenwood Canyon, it was diverted to the other side of the river and through a tunnel, just to protect this scenic and popular area. A sign at the parking area warns that the trail is difficult, be prepared—have water and sturdy shoes for hiking, no dogs allowed on the trail, no fishing or swimming in the lake.

An early morning look at the beauty of Hanging Lake, one of the area's most visited attractions.

The climb to the lake is steep and rocky. The narrow trail gets very crowded, so it's best to go during the week, and preferably very early in the morning. The route is marked with ¼-mile posts, which help give a sense of how much farther you have to go to the lake (total distance is 1.2 miles). This hike can also be accessed by the Glenwood Canyon Bike Path, which runs right past the trailhead. Make sure to bring your camera—Hanging Lake is probably one of the most scenic sights in all of Colorado.

Directions to Trailhead: Take I-70 east from Glenwood Springs just over 8 miles to Exit 125, the Hanging Lake Exit, and park. From the parking area you walk east ¼ mile on the concrete Glenwood Canyon Bike Path to the trailhead on the left, just before Deadhorse Creek.

Trail Route: The trail goes up to the left of the creek, relatively steeply. Ahead on the right is a sheer rock face. In about 6–7 minutes you cross the first of six bridges over Dead Horse Creek. You're heading up through a beautiful narrow gorge with huge rocks everywhere, and a cascading creek flowing alongside. Just beyond the second bridge you come to a trail junction, with a sign showing Hanging Lake (Trail) #1853 straight ahead, and Dead Horse (Trail) #1851 to the right. Stay straight and you will immediately pass the ¼-mile post. Proceed along the steep rocky trail, the stream cascading in numerous small waterfalls alongside, high rocky walls rising on both sides.

At ½ mile, at the third bridge, the stream drops as a waterfall right above the bridge. The continued steep ascent contains a couple of spots where the trail levels a bit to give you a breather. Between the fourth and fifth bridges is a small wooden shelter on the left. After encountering more waterfalls, shortly before the lake it is necessary to make a final steep ascent up stair-like rocks, with a pipe railing alongside for safety's sake. It's narrow here, and you may have to wait on other people when it's crowded.

Right above this section you come to the boardwalk over the creek and around the lake (to protect the fragile ecosystem). Just before the boardwalk a trail goes up to the left with a sign "Spouting Rock". (To get to Spouting Rock, go up the trail for about 3 minutes. You come to a pool surrounded by rock, with a 75-foot waterfall coming down over the top of the rock behind the pool, as well as water spouting out of two holes in the rock—a triple waterfall. You can get under the waterfall to cool off if necessary as the mist surrounds you.) A series of waterfalls pour down behind the lake, and rock walls rise around the lake. Hanging Lake is a very crystal clear blue-green, and many trout can be seen swimming around. It's truly a mystical setting.

Index

A

American Lake, 41–42, 44
American Lake Trailhead, 41
Anaerobic Nightmare Trail, 59, 61
Anderson Creek, 20
Anderson Lake, 19–21
Arbaney–Kittle Trail, 69–72
Arkansas Mountain, 97
Ashcroft, 29, 41–43
Aspen Art Museum, 30
Aspen Business Center, 31
Aspen Club, 32
Aspen Mountain, 11, 31–32, 39
Aspen Recreation Center, 58–61
Assignation Creek, 91
Assignation Ridge, 85, 90–91
Avalanche Campground, 93
Avalanche Creek, 64, 93–94, 96
Avalanche Creek Trail, 93–94
Avalanche Creek Trailhead, 94
Avalanche Lake, 93
Avalanche Pass, 96–97

B

Basalt, 30–31, 64, 69–74, 77,
    79–80, 82, 85, 88
Basalt Mountain, 71
Bear Creek, 66–68
Bear Creek Falls, 66
Beaver Lake, 97–98
Benedict Bridge, 34–36, 40
Blue Ribbon Trail, 87
Braille Trail, 9, 15–16
Bridal Veil Falls, 110
Brooklyn Gulch, 17
Brush Creek, 31

Brush Creek Trail, 58
Brush Creek Valley, 61
Buck Creek, 100–1
Buck Creek Basin, 100–1
Buckskin Basin, 96–97
Buckskin Pass, 29, 46–48
Buckskin Peak, 55

C

Capitol Creek, 62–64
Capitol Creek Loop, 62–64
Capitol Creek Trail, 62
Capitol Creek Trailhead, 62–63, 65
Capitol Creek Valley, 51, 62, 65
Capitol Ditch Trail, 62–63
Capitol Ditch Trailhead, 62
Capitol Lake, 51, 62–64
Capitol Peak, 43–44, 46, 51, 57,
    62–66, 68, 71, 75, 95–97
Capone, Al, 104
Carbonate Creek Basin, 97
Carbondale, 5, 69, 85–88, 90–93,
    95, 97–98, 100
Carter Basin, 78
Carter Basin Trail, 77
Carter Lake, 79
Cascades, 13–14
Castle Creek Valley, 41–42
Castle Peak, 43–44
Cathedral Lake, 42–44
Cathedral Lake Trail, 44
Cathedral Lake Trailhead, 42
Cathedral Peak, 43–44
Cemetery Hill, 104
Chair Mountain, 85, 100–1
Coffeepot Park, 75, 78
Coleman Creek, 22

Collegiate Peaks, 77
Collegiate Peaks Wilderness, 7,
    11–13, 16, 18, 26
Colorado Midland Railroad, 69
Colorado River, 105
Connector Trail, 54
Continental Divide, 5, 9, 18–19,
    21–24, 26–27, 69, 82–83
Conundrum Peak, 44
Conundrum Valley, 44
Crater Lake, 45–49
Crater Lake Trail, 45–46, 48
Crested Butte, 99
Crystal (see Crystal City)
Crystal City, 85, 97–99
Crystal Mill, 85, 99
Crystal River, 93, 97–98
Crystal River Valley, 5, 85–87, 91,
    96, 98

D

Deadhorse Creek, 111
Deadhorse Trail, 111
"Deadly Bells", 46, 48
Deadman Gulch, 25
Deer Mountain, 83
Denver & Rio Grande Railroad, 29
Devil's Rockpile, 99
Diemer Lake, 80
Difficult Campground, 11
Difficult Creek, 11–12
Difficult Trail, 9, 11–12
Dinkle Lake, 88
Discovery Trail, 9, 15–16
Ditch Trail, 51–55
Doc Holliday, 103–4
Doc Holliday's grave, 103–4
Doc Holliday Trail, 103–4
Duley Park, 93–94

E

East Brush Creek, 59, 61
East Creek, 94–95
East Creek Trail, 94–96
East No Name Creek, 108
East Snowmass Creek, 54–55
East Snowmass Creek Basin, 54
East Snowmass Creek Valley, 54
East Snowmass Pass, 55
East Snowmass Trail, 51, 53–55
Electric Pass, 42–44
El Jebel, 72
Elk Mountain Range, 27, 43, 48,
    64, 71, 75, 94, 96–97, 108
Elk Mountains, 21, 35, 37–39
Elk Mountains Ridge, 64–65, 71
Elk Wallow Campground, 77
"erratic boulders", 14

F

Fairy Caves, 103
Flattops Wilderness, 103, 106
Fravert Basin, 99
Frenchman Creek, 74
Frontier Historical Museum, 104
Fryingpan Lakes, 80, 82–83
Fryingpan Lakes Trailhead, 82
Fryingpan River, 69, 77, 79–80, 82
Fryingpan River Valley, 5, 69, 71,
    74, 78, 80, 82

G

Geneva Lake, 98–100
Geneva Lake Trail, 98
Gentlemen's Ridge, 31
giardia, 6
Gift Creek, 96
Glenwood Canyon, 5, 103, 106,
    110–11
Glenwood Canyon Bike Path, 111

Glenwood Cemetery, 104
Glenwood Hot Springs, 103–4
Glenwood Springs, 5, 69, 88,
    103–8, 111
Golay, Jeanne, 105
Gore Range, 64
Government Trail, 51, 58–61
Grizzly Creek, 18–19, 106–9
Grizzly Creek Trail, 103, 108–9
Grizzly Creek Trailhead, 108
Grizzly Creek Valley, 27
Grizzly Lake, 18–19
Grizzly Lake Trail, 18
Grizzly Lake Trailhead, 18
Grizzly Peak, 18–19, 27
Grizzly Reservoir, 18, 20
Grottos, 9, 13–14

H

Hagerman Pass, 69, 80
Hagerman Peak, 67, 96, 100
Hanging Lake, 110–11
Hanging Lake Trail, 103, 110–11
Hanging Lake Trailhead, 110
Hardscrabble Lake, 65
Hawk Mountain, 96
Hayden Peak, 39, 44
Hay Park, 89
Hell Roaring Creek, 64, 93–94
Hell Roaring Trail, 64–66, 93–94
Hell Roaring Trailhead, 64–65
Henderson Park, 75, 78
Henderson Park Trailhead, 75, 77
Henry Stein Park (see Stein Park)
Herron Park, 29–30
Holland Hills, 69, 71–72
Holliday, Doc (see Doc Holliday)
Holy Cross Wilderness, 7, 69, 75,
    78–79
Horse Ranch, 56–58

Hunter Creek, 30, 34–37, 40
Hunter Creek–Smuggler Loop,
    34–37
Hunter Creek Trail, 34, 40
Hunter Creek Trailhead, 35–36, 38
Hunter Creek Trail Parking Lot, 34
Hunter–Fryingpan Wilderness, 7,
    21–23, 69, 82
Hunter Valley, 29, 34–38
Hunter Valley Trail, 37–38, 40

I

"ice caves", 13
Independence, 9, 11, 22, 24, 27
Independence Lake, 23–24
Independence Pass, 5, 9, 11,
    21–23, 26, 32
Iowa Shaft, 37
Iselin Park, 59–61
Ivanhoe Creek, 80, 82
Ivanhoe Lake, 80

J

Jack Creek, 25
Jeanne Golay Trail, 105
Jeanne Golay Trailhead, 105
Jess Weaver Trail, 103, 106–8
Jess Weaver Trailhead, 106–7
Josephine Lake, 75–78

K

Krabloonik, 52–54, 67

L

Lani White Trail, 36, 40
Larson Peak, 21
Last Chance, 78
Lead King Basin, 97–99
Leadville, 9, 14, 26, 69
Lily Lake Trail, 95
Lincoln Creek, 9, 14, 17

Lincoln Creek Road, 17–20
Lincoln Creek Valley, 19, 27
Linkins Lake, 22–24
Linkins Lake Trail, 22–24
Linkins Lake Trailhead, 22–23
Little Gem Lake, 100
Lost Man basin, 25
Lost Man Campground, 21, 24–25
Lost Man Creek, 23, 25
Lost Man drainage, 24
Lost Man Lake, 23–25
Lost Man Loop, 23–25
Lost Man Reservoir, 24–25
Lost Man Trail, 23–25
Lost Man Trailhead, 21, 23
Lower Savage Lake, 79
Lyle Lake, 79–81
Lyle Lake Trailhead, 79–80

M

Marble, 5, 84, 97–98
Maroon Bells, 29, 44–49, 95–96, 100, 108
Maroon Bells–Snowmass Wilderness, 7, 41–43, 45–46, 48, 51, 54, 64, 66, 85, 88, 93–94, 96, 98
Maroon Creek, 61
Maroon Creek Valley, 59–61
Maroon Lake, 29, 45–48, 51
Maroon Peak, 43
Maroon–Snowmass Trail, 47, 66–68
Maroon–Snowmass Trailhead, 66
Marten Creek, 82
McClure Pass, 5, 85, 100
Midway Pass, 21–22, 40
Midway Trail, 21, 25, 40
Minnehaha Gulch, 47
Morman Creek, 81

Morman Lake, 78–81
Mountain Valley, 32
Mount Daly, 39, 44, 46, 54, 57, 62–64, 66, 71, 75, 95–97
Mount Massive, 81
Mount Oklahoma, 83
Mount Sopris, 32, 37, 39, 57, 69, 71–72, 75, 85–91, 104–5
Muddy Creek, 101
Mushroom Rock, 85–87
Mushroom Rock Trail, 86–87

N

Nature Trail, 52–53
New York Creek, 16–17
New York Creek Diversion, 17
New York Creek Pass, 16
New York Creek Trail, 16–17
New York Creek Trailhead, 16
New York Peak, 17
New York Trail #2182, 17
No Name Creek, 106–9
No Name Trail, 106
North Fork Lost Creek, 97
North Fork River, 100
North Lost Trail, 97
North Lost Trail Trailhead, 96
North Maroon Peak, 43, 47
North Thompson Creek, 89–90

O

Old Snowmass (see Snowmass)

P

Peak 12,812, 27
Peak 13,045, 27
Peak 13,198, 27
Perham Creek, 91
Perham Creek Trail, 90–91
Perham Creek Trailhead, 90

Petroleum Lake, 19–21
Petroleum Lake Trailhead, 19
Pierre Lakes, 68
Pine Creek, 42–43
Pioneer Cemetery, 103–4
Pioneer Cemetery Trailhead, 103
"Platform", 32–33, 37
"Plunge", 40
Portal Campground, 20
Puppy Smith, 29–30
Pyramid Peak, 39, 43–44, 46,
   95–96

R

Ragged Mountain Trail, 85, 100–1
Ragged Mountain Trailhead, 100
Ragged Peak, 100–1
Raggeds Trail #820, 101
Raggeds Wilderness, 85
Red Hill, 74, 86
Red Hill Recreation Area, 86
Red Mountain, 29, 34, 36, 38–39,
   103, 105
Red Mountain Trail, 105
Redstone, 5, 85, 95–96, 98, 100
Redstone Castle, 85, 98
Redstone Inn, 85, 98
Red Table Mountain, 74–75
"reservoir bridge", 35, 37
RFOV, 63
Rim Trail, 51, 56–58
Rio Grande Trail, 29–31, 38–40
Roaring Fork drainage, 24
Roaring Fork Overlook, 13
rock fins, 89
Rock Garden, 60–61
Rocky Fork Creek, 73
Rocky Fork Day Use Area, 73
Rocky Fork Trail, 72–73
Roosevelt, Teddy, 104

Ruedi Creek, 74
Ruedi Creek Campgrounds, 74
Ruedi Dam, 72–73, 75
Ruedi Overlook Trail, 74–75
Ruedi Reservoir, 69, 73–75
Ruedi Trail, 74

S

Savage Lakes, 78–79
Savage Lakes Trail, 78–79
Savage Lakes Trailhead, 78–79
Savage Mountain, 77–78
Sawatch Range, 75
Scenic Route Trail, 46, 48
Schofield Pass, 99
Schwartz, J. C., 104
Sellar Lake, 80
Shadyside Trail, 39–40
Shoemaker, Len, 43
Silver Queen Gondola, 31
Slaughterhouse Bridge, 30, 38, 40
Sleigh Ride Trail, 51–55
Smuggler Mine, 32–33, 37
Smuggler Mountain, 29, 32–37, 46
Smuggler Mountain Road, 32–33,
   37
Snowmass, 51, 63–64, 67
Snowmass Creek, 54, 66, 68
Snowmass Creek Trail, 51, 66–68
Snowmass Creek Trailhead, 66
Snowmass Creek Valley, 54, 68
Snowmass Lake, 46, 51, 66–68,
   100
Snowmass Mountain, 43–44, 51,
   67–68, 71, 77, 95–96, 99–100
Snowmass Peak, 67, 96, 100
Snowmass Village, 51–61, 67
Snowmass Village Mall, 52–53,
   55, 67
Sopris, Richard, 104

South Fork Pass, 25
South Thompson Creek, 90–91
Spouting Rock, 110–11
Stein Park, 29–30, 38–40
Stein Trail, 31
Sunnyside–Hunter Valley Loop, 38–40
Sunnyside Trail, 38–40
Sunnyside Trailhead, 38, 40

T

Tenth Mountain Bridge, 35, 37, 40
Thimble Rock, 35
Thomas Lakes, 69, 85, 88–89
Thomas Lakes Trailhead, 88
Thompson Creek, 89–90
Thompson Creek Trail, 89–90
Tiehack Bridge, 59, 61
Tomb of the Unknown Soldier, 85
Trail Rider Pass, 100
Triangle Peak, 31
Twin Lakes, 26

U

Upper Capitol Creek Trail, 63
Upper Meadows, 17
Ute Trail, 29, 31–32

Ute Trailhead, 31

V

Volunteers for Outdoor Colorado, 63

W

Warren Lakes, 33
Weaver, Jess, 108
Weller Campground, 12, 14
Weller Lake, 9, 12–13
West Government Trail, 54
West Maroon Pass, 29, 48–49
West Maroon Trail, 46–47, 49
West Maroon Valley, 49
West Snowmass Trail, 63, 68
Whites Lake, 61
Wildcat Ranch, 56–57
Wildcat Reservoir, 57–58
Wilderness Act of 1964, 7
Williams Lake, 65–66
Williams Mountains, 21–22, 35, 64
Willow Lake, 47
Willow Pass, 47
Woody Creek, 30–31, 71–72

Y

Yule Creek, 98

Notes

Notes

Notes